'I read *The Checklist Manifesto* in one sitting yesterday, which is an amazing tribute to the book that Gawande has crafted. Not only is the book loaded with fascinating stories, but it honestly changed the way I think about the world. It is the best book I've read in ages' Steven Levitt, author of *Freakonomics*

'A riveting and thought provoking book' David Aaronovitch, *The Times*

'Gawande deftly weaves in examples of checklist successes in diverse fields like aviation and skyscraper construction … fascinating reading' *New York Times Book Review*

'Both a meditation on the growing complexity of the world and a how to book on coping with that complexity' *Economist*

'Real life surgical drama is Gawande's first passion and the subject of his two previous, highly successful books. He has an instinctive sense of how much jargon the lay reader will tolerate – how to maintain the balance between accessibility and precision. He manages to be vivid without being gruesome … Gawande's style is always clear, with a crispy lilt' *Observer*

'Gawande is a writer with a scalpel pen and an X-ray eye. Diagnosis: riveting' *Time*

'Gawande's powerful and readable book *The Checklist Manifesto* explains how to cut through the complexity of modern life' *Scottish Sunday Post*

D1082430

'In developing his ideas about checklists, Gawande explores the methodologies of building skyscrapers and flying jet aircrafts in emergencies as well as of surgical teams. He is a superb reporter, blending anecdotes and deep research in vivid and stylish prose' *Sydney Morning Herald*

'Even skeptical readers will find the evidence staggering ... thoughtfully written and soundly defended, this book calls for medical professionals to improve patient care by adopting a basic, common sense approach' *Washington Post*

'This is a brilliant book about an idea so simple it sounds dumb until you hear the case for it. Atul Gawande presents an argument so strong that I challenge anyone to go away from this book unconvinced' *Seattle Times*

'The scope goes well beyond medicine ... read this book and you might find yourself making checklists for the most mundane tasks – and be better off for it' *Business Week*

ATUL GAWANDE is the author of the international bestseller *Being Mortal*, *Better* and *Complications* and a staff writer for the *New Yorker*. A MacArthur fellow, a general and endocrine surgeon at the Brigham and Women's Hospital in Boston and an associate professor at Harvard Medical School and the Harvard School of Public Health, he also leads the World Health Organisations Safe Surgery Saves Lives Program. He lives with his wife and three children in Massachusetts.

THE CHECKLIST MANIFESTO

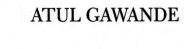

ATUL GAWANDE

THE CHECKLIST MANIFESTO HOW TO GET THINGS RIGHT

PROFILE BOOKS

This paperback edition published in 2011

First published in Great Britain in 2010 by
PROFILE BOOKS LTD
3A Exmouth House
Pine Street
London EC1R 0JH
www.profilebooks.com

First published in America in 2009 by
Metropolitan Books of Henry Holt and Company LLC

Some material in this book originally appeared
in the *New Yorker* essay, 'The Checklist' in different form

11

Printed and bound by CPI Group (UK) Ltd,
Croydon, CR0 4YY

A CIP catalogue record for this book is available from the British Library.

ISBN 978 1 84668 314 5
eISBN 978 1 84765 187 7

For Hunter, Hattie, and Walker

CONTENTS

INTRODUCTION   I

1. THE PROBLEM OF EXTREME COMPLEXITY   15

2. THE CHECKLIST   32

3. THE END OF THE MASTER BUILDER   48

4. THE IDEA   72

5. THE FIRST TRY   86

6. THE CHECKLIST FACTORY   114

7. THE TEST   136

8. THE HERO IN THE AGE OF CHECKLISTS   158

9. THE SAVE   187

NOTES ON SOURCES   195

ACKNOWLEDGMENTS   205

THE CHECKLIST MANIFESTO

INTRODUCTION

I was chatting with a medical school friend of mine who is now a general surgeon in San Francisco. We were trading war stories, as surgeons are apt to do. One of John's was about a guy who came in on Halloween night with a stab wound. He had been at a costume party. He got into an altercation. And now here he was.

He was stable, breathing normally, not in pain, just drunk and babbling to the trauma team. They cut off his clothes with shears and looked him over from head to toe, front and back. He was of moderate size, about two hundred pounds, most of the excess around his middle. That was where they found the stab wound, a neat two-inch red slit in his belly, pouting open like a fish mouth. A thin mustard yellow strip of omental fat tongued out of it—fat from inside his abdomen, not the pale yellow, superficial fat that lies beneath the skin. They'd need to take him to the operating room, check to make sure the bowel wasn't injured, and sew up the little gap.

"No big deal," John said.

If it were a bad injury, they'd need to crash into the operating room—stretcher flying, nurses racing to get the surgical equipment set up, the anesthesiologists skipping their detailed review of the medical records. But this was not a bad injury. They had time, they determined. The patient lay waiting on his stretcher in the stucco-walled trauma bay while the OR was readied.

Then a nurse noticed he'd stopped babbling. His heart rate had skyrocketed. His eyes were rolling back in his head. He didn't respond when she shook him. She called for help, and the members of the trauma team swarmed back into the room. His blood pressure was barely detectible. They stuck a tube down his airway and pushed air into his lungs, poured fluid and emergency-release blood into him. Still they couldn't get his pressure up.

So now they *were* crashing into the operating room—stretcher flying, nurses racing to get the surgical equipment set up, the anesthesiologists skipping their review of the records, a resident splashing a whole bottle of Betadine antiseptic onto his belly, John grabbing a fat No. 10 blade and slicing down through the skin of the man's abdomen in one clean, determined swipe from rib cage to pubis.

"Cautery."

He drew the electrified metal tip of the cautery pen along the fat underneath the skin, parting it in a line from top to bottom, then through the fibrous white sheath of fascia between the abdominal muscles. He pierced his way into the abdominal cavity itself, and suddenly an ocean of blood burst out of the patient.

"Crap."

The blood was everywhere. The assailant's knife had gone more than a foot through the man's skin, through the fat, through the muscle, past the intestine, along the left of his spinal column, and right into the aorta, the main artery from the heart.

"Which was crazy," John said. Another surgeon joined to help and got a fist down on the aorta, above the puncture point. That stopped the worst of the bleeding and they began to get control of the situation. John's colleague said he hadn't seen an injury like it since Vietnam.

The description was pretty close, it turned out. The other guy at the costume party, John later learned, was dressed as a soldier—with a bayonet.

The patient was touch and go for a couple days. But he pulled through. John still shakes his head ruefully when he talks about the case.

There are a thousand ways that things can go wrong when you've got a patient with a stab wound. But everyone involved got almost every step right—the head-to-toe examination, the careful tracking of the patient's blood pressure and pulse and rate of breathing, the monitoring of his consciousness, the fluids run in by IV, the call to the blood bank to have blood ready, the placement of a urinary catheter to make sure his urine was running clear, everything. Except no one remembered to ask the patient or the emergency medical technicians what the weapon was.

"Your mind doesn't think of a bayonet in San Francisco," John could only say.

He told me about another patient, who was undergoing an operation to remove a cancer of his stomach when his heart suddenly stopped.* John remembered looking up at the cardiac monitor and saying to the anesthesiologist, "Hey, is that asystole?" Asystole is total cessation of heart function. It looks like a flat line on the monitor, as if the monitor is not even hooked up to the patient.

The anesthesiologist said, "A lead must have fallen off," because it seemed impossible to believe that the patient's heart had stopped. The man was in his late forties and had been perfectly healthy. The tumor was found almost by chance. He had gone to see his physician about something else, a cough perhaps, and mentioned he'd been having some heartburn, too. Well, not heartburn exactly. He felt like food sometimes got stuck in his esophagus and wouldn't go down and *that* gave him heartburn. The doctor ordered an imaging test that required him to swallow a milky barium drink while standing in front of an X-ray machine. And there on the images it was: a fleshy mouse-size mass, near the top of the stomach, intermittently pressing up against the entrance like a stopper. It had been caught early. There were no signs of spread. The only known cure was surgery, in this case a total gastrectomy, meaning removal of his entire stomach, a major four-hour undertaking.

The team members were halfway through the procedure. The cancer was out. There'd been no problems whatsoever. They were getting ready to reconstruct the patient's digestive tract when the monitor went flat-line. It took them about five

*Identifying details were changed at John's request.

seconds to figure out that a lead had not fallen off. The anesthesiologist could feel no pulse in the patient's carotid artery. His heart had stopped.

John tore the sterile drapes off the patient and started doing chest compressions, the patient's intestines bulging in and out of his open abdomen with each push. A nurse called a Code Blue.

John paused here in telling the story and asked me to suppose I was in his situation. "So, now, what would you do?"

I tried to think it through. The asystole happened in the midst of major surgery. Therefore, massive blood loss would be at the top of my list. I would open fluids wide, I said, and look for bleeding.

That's what the anesthesiologist said, too. But John had the patient's abdomen completely open. There was no bleeding, and he told the anesthesiologist so.

"He couldn't believe it," John said. "He kept saying, 'There must be massive bleeding! There must be massive bleeding!'" But there was none.

Lack of oxygen was also a possibility. I said I'd put the oxygen at 100 percent and check the airway. I'd also draw blood and send it for stat laboratory tests to rule out unusual abnormalities.

John said they thought of that, too. The airway was fine. And as for the lab tests, they would take at least twenty minutes to get results, by which point it would be too late.

Could it be a collapsed lung—a pneumothorax? There were no signs of it. They listened with a stethoscope and heard good air movement on both sides of the chest.

The cause therefore had to be a pulmonary embolism, I said—a blood clot must have traveled to the patient's heart and plugged off his circulation. It's rare, but patients with cancer undergoing major surgery are at risk, and if it happens there's not much that can be done. One could give a bolus of epinephrine—adrenalin—to try to jump-start the heart, but it wouldn't likely do much good.

John said that his team had come to the same conclusion. After fifteen minutes of pumping up and down on the patient's chest, the line on the screen still flat as death, the situation seemed hopeless. Among those who arrived to help, however, was a senior anesthesiologist who had been in the room when the patient was being put to sleep. When he left, nothing seemed remotely off-kilter. He kept thinking to himself, someone must have done something wrong.

He asked the anesthesiologist in the room if he had done any-thing different in the fifteen minutes before the cardiac arrest.

No. Wait. Yes. The patient had had a low potassium level on routine labs that were sent during the first part of the case, when all otherwise seemed fine, and the anesthesiologist had given him a dose of potassium to correct it.

I was chagrined at having missed this possibility. An abnormal level of potassium is a classic cause of asystole. It's mentioned in every textbook. I couldn't believe I overlooked it. Severely low potassium levels can stop the heart, in which case a corrective dose of potassium is the remedy. And too much potassium can stop the heart, as well—that's how states execute prisoners.

The senior anesthesiologist asked to see the potassium bag that had been hanging. Someone fished it out of the trash and that was when they figured it out. The anesthesiologist had used the wrong concentration of potassium, a concentration one hundred times higher than he'd intended. He had, in other words, given the patient a lethal overdose of potassium.

After so much time, it wasn't clear whether the patient could be revived. It might well have been too late. But from that point on, they did everything they were supposed to do. They gave injections of insulin and glucose to lower the toxic potassium level. Knowing that the medications would take a good fifteen minutes to kick in—way too long—they also gave intravenous calcium and inhaled doses of a drug called albuterol, which act more quickly. The potassium levels dropped rapidly. And the patient's heartbeat did indeed come back.

The surgical team was so shaken they weren't sure they could finish the operation. They'd not only nearly killed the man but also failed to recognize how. They did finish the procedure, though. John went out and told the family what had happened. He and the patient were lucky. The man recovered—almost as if the whole episode had never occurred.

The stories surgeons tell one another are often about the shock of the unexpected—the bayonet in San Francisco, the cardiac arrest when all seemed fine—and sometimes about regret over missed possibilities. We talk about our great saves but also about our great failures, and we all have them. They are part of what we do. We like to think of ourselves as in control. But John's stories got me thinking about what is really in our control and what is not.

In the 1970s, the philosophers Samuel Gorovitz and Alasdair MacIntyre published a short essay on the nature of human fallibility that I read during my surgical training and haven't stopped pondering since. The question they sought to answer was why we fail at what we set out to do in the world. One reason, they observed, is "necessary fallibility"—some things we want to do are simply beyond our capacity. We are not omniscient or all-powerful. Even enhanced by technology, our physical and mental powers are limited. Much of the world and universe is—and will remain—outside our understanding and control.

There are substantial realms, however, in which control is within our reach. We can build skyscrapers, predict snowstorms, save people from heart attacks and stab wounds. In such realms, Gorovitz and MacIntyre point out, we have just two reasons that we may nonetheless fail.

The first is ignorance—we may err because science has given us only a partial understanding of the world and how it works. There are skyscrapers we do not yet know how to build, snowstorms we cannot predict, heart attacks we still haven't learned how to stop. The second type of failure the philosophers call ineptitude—because in these instances the knowledge exists, yet we fail to apply it correctly. This is the skyscraper that is built wrong and collapses, the snowstorm whose signs the meteorologist just plain missed, the stab wound from a weapon the doctors forgot to ask about.

Thinking about John's cases as a small sample of the difficulties we face in early-twenty-first-century medicine, I was struck by how greatly the balance of ignorance and ineptitude has shifted. For nearly all of history, people's lives have been governed primarily by ignorance. This was nowhere more clear than with the illnesses that befell us. We knew little about what caused them or what could be done to remedy them. But sometime over the last several decades—and it is only over the last several decades—science has filled in enough knowledge to make ineptitude as much our struggle as ignorance.

Consider heart attacks. Even as recently as the 1950s, we had little idea of how to prevent or treat them. We didn't know, for example, about the danger of high blood pressure, and had we been aware of it we wouldn't have known what to do about it. The first safe medication to treat hypertension was not developed and conclusively demonstrated to prevent disease until the 1960s. We didn't know about the role of cholesterol, either, or genetics or smoking or diabetes.

Furthermore, if someone had a heart attack, we had little idea of how to treat it. We'd give some morphine for the pain, perhaps some oxygen, and put the patient on strict bed rest for weeks—patients weren't even permitted to get up and go to the bathroom for fear of stressing their damaged hearts. Then everyone would pray and cross their fingers and hope the patient would make it out of the hospital to spend the rest of his or her life at home as a cardiac cripple.

Today, by contrast, we have at least a dozen effective ways to reduce your likelihood of having a heart attack—for instance, controlling your blood pressure, prescribing a statin to lower cholesterol and inflammation, limiting blood sugar levels, encouraging exercise regularly, helping with smoking cessation, and, if there are early signs of heart disease, getting you to a cardiologist for still further recommendations. If you should have a heart attack, we have a whole panel of effective therapies that can not only save your life but also limit the damage to your heart: we have clot-busting drugs that can reopen your blocked coronary arteries; we have cardiac catheters that can balloon them open; we have open heart surgery techniques that let us bypass the obstructed vessels; and we've learned that in some instances all we really have to do is send you to bed with some oxygen, an aspirin, a statin, and blood pressure medications—in a couple days you'll generally be ready to go home and gradually back to your usual life.

But now the problem we face is ineptitude, or maybe it's "eptitude"—making sure we apply the knowledge we have consistently and correctly. Just making the right treatment choice among the many options for a heart attack patient can be difficult, even for expert clinicians. Furthermore, whatever the chosen treatment, each involves abundant complexities and pitfalls. Careful studies have shown, for example, that heart attack patients undergoing cardiac balloon therapy should have it done within ninety minutes of arrival at a hospital. After that, survival falls off sharply. In practical terms this means that, within ninety minutes, medical teams must complete all their testing for every patient who turns up in an emergency room with chest pain, make a correct diagnosis and plan, discuss the decision with the patient, obtain his or her agreement to proceed, confirm there are no allergies or medical problems that have to be accounted for, ready a cath lab and team, transport the patient, and get started.

What is the likelihood that all this will actually occur within ninety minutes in an average hospital? In 2006, it was less than 50 percent.

This is not an unusual example. These kinds of failures are routine in medicine. Studies have found that at least 30 percent of patients with stroke receive incomplete or inappropriate care from their doctors, as do 45 percent of patients with asthma and 60 percent of patients with pneumonia. Getting the steps right is proving brutally hard, even if you know them.

I have been trying for some time to understand the source of our greatest difficulties and stresses in medicine. It is not money or government or the threat of malpractice lawsuits or insurance company hassles—although they all play their role. It is the complexity that science has dropped upon us and the enormous strains we are encountering in making good on its promise. The problem is not uniquely American; I have seen it everywhere—in Europe, in Asia, in rich countries and poor. Moreover, I have found to my surprise that the challenge is not limited to medicine.

Know-how and sophistication have increased remarkably across almost all our realms of endeavor, and as a result so has our struggle to deliver on them. You see it in the frequent mistakes authorities make when hurricanes or tornadoes or other disasters hit. You see it in the 36 percent increase between 2004 and 2007 in lawsuits against attorneys for legal mistakes—the most common being simple administrative errors, like missed calendar dates and clerical screwups, as well as errors in applying the law. You see it in flawed software design, in foreign intelligence failures, in our tottering banks—in fact, in almost any endeavor requiring mastery of complexity and of large amounts of knowledge.

Such failures carry an emotional valence that seems to cloud how we think about them. Failures of ignorance we can forgive. If the knowledge of the best thing to do in a given situation does not exist, we are happy to have people simply make their best effort. But if the knowledge exists and is not applied correctly, it is difficult not to be infuriated. What do you mean half of heart attack patients don't get their treatment on time? What do you mean that two-thirds of death penalty cases are overturned because of errors? It is not for nothing that the philosophers gave these failures so unmerciful a name—*ineptitude*. Those on the receiving end use other words, like *negligence* or even *heart-lessness*.

For those who do the work, however—for those who care for the patients, practice the law, respond when need calls—the judgment feels like it ignores how extremely difficult the job is. Every day there is more and more to manage and get right and learn. And defeat under conditions of complexity occurs far more often despite great effort rather than from a lack of it. That's why the traditional solution in most professions has not been to punish failure but instead to encourage more experience and training.

There can be no disputing the importance of experience. It is not enough for a surgeon to have the textbook knowledge of how to treat trauma victims—to understand the science of penetrating wounds, the damage they cause, the different approaches to diagnosis and treatment, the importance of acting quickly. One must also grasp the clinical reality, with its nuances of timing and sequence. One needs practice to achieve mastery, a body of experience before one achieves real success. And if what we are missing when we fail is individual skill, then what is needed is simply more training and practice.

But what is striking about John's cases is that he is among the best-trained surgeons I know, with more than a decade on the front lines. And this is the common pattern. The capability of individuals is not proving to be our primary difficulty, whether in medicine or elsewhere. Far from it. Training in most fields is longer and more intense than ever. People spend years of sixty-, seventy-, eighty-hour weeks building their base of knowledge and experience before going out into practice on their own—whether they are doctors or professors or lawyers or engineers. They have sought to perfect themselves. It is not clear how we could produce substantially more expertise than we already have. Yet our failures remain frequent. They persist despite remarkable individual ability.

Here, then, is our situation at the start of the twenty-first century: We have accumulated stupendous know-how. We have put it in the hands of some of the most highly trained, highly skilled, and hardworking people in our society. And, with it, they have indeed accomplished extraordinary things. Nonetheless, that know-how is often unmanageable. Avoidable failures are common and per- sistent, not to mention demoralizing and frustrating, across many fields—from medicine to finance, business to government. And the reason is increasingly evident: the volume and complexity of what we know has exceeded our individual ability to deliver its benefits correctly, safely, or reliably. Knowledge has both saved us and burdened us.

That means we need a different strategy for overcoming fail- ure, one that builds on experience and takes advantage of the knowledge people have but somehow also makes up for our inevitable human inadequacies. And there is such a strategy— though it will seem almost ridiculous in its simplicity, maybe even crazy to those of us who have spent years carefully develop- ing ever more advanced skills and technologies.

It is a checklist.

1. THE PROBLEM OF EXTREME COMPLEXITY

Some time ago I read a case report in the *Annals of Thoracic Surgery*. It was, in the dry prose of a medical journal article, the story of a nightmare. In a small Austrian town in the Alps, a mother and father had been out on a walk in the woods with their three-year-old daughter. The parents lost sight of the girl for a moment and that was all it took. She fell into an icy fishpond. The parents frantically jumped in after her. But she was lost beneath the surface for thirty minutes before they finally found her on the pond bottom. They pulled her to the surface and got her to the shore. Following instructions from an emergency response team reached on their cell phone, they began cardiopulmonary resuscitation.

Rescue personnel arrived eight minutes later and took the first recordings of the girl's condition. She was unresponsive. She had no blood pressure or pulse or sign of breathing. Her body temperature was just 66 degrees. Her pupils were dilated and unreactive to light, indicating cessation of brain function. She was gone.

But the emergency technicians continued CPR anyway. A helicopter took her to the nearest hospital, where she was wheeled directly into an operating room, a member of the emergency crew straddling her on the gurney, pumping her chest. A surgical team got her onto a heart-lung bypass machine as rapidly as it could. The surgeon had to cut down through the skin of the child's right groin and sew one of the desk-size machine's silicone rubber tubes into her femoral vein to take the blood out of her, then another into her femoral artery to send the blood back. A perfusionist turned the pump on, and as he adjusted the oxygen and temperature and flow through the system, the clear tubing turned maroon with her blood. Only then did they stop the girl's chest compressions.

Between the transport time and the time it took to plug the machine into her, she had been lifeless for an hour and a half. By the two-hour mark, however, her body temperature had risen almost ten degrees, and her heart began to beat. It was her first organ to come back.

After six hours, the girl's core reached 98.6 degrees, normal body temperature. The team tried to shift her from the bypass machine to a mechanical ventilator, but the pond water and debris had damaged her lungs too severely for the oxygen pumped in through the breathing tube to reach her blood. So they switched her instead to an artificial-lung system known as ECMO—extracorporeal membrane oxygenation. To do this, the surgeons had to open her chest down the middle with a power saw and sew the lines to and from the portable ECMO unit directly into her aorta and her beating heart.

The ECMO machine now took over. The surgeons removed the heart-lung bypass machine tubing. They repaired the vessels and closed her groin incision. The surgical team moved the girl into intensive care, with her chest still open and covered with sterile plastic foil. Through the day and night, the intensive care unit team worked on suctioning the water and debris from her lungs with a fiberoptic bronchoscope. By the next day, her lungs had recovered sufficiently for the team to switch her from ECMO to a mechanical ventilator, which required taking her back to the operating room to unplug the tubing, repair the holes, and close her chest.

Over the next two days, all the girl's organs recovered—her liver, her kidneys, her intestines, everything except her brain. A CT scan showed global brain swelling, which is a sign of diffuse damage, but no actual dead zones. So the team escalated the care one step further. It drilled a hole into the girl's skull, threaded a probe into the brain to monitor the pressure, and kept that pressure tightly controlled through constant adjustments in her fluids and medications. For more than a week, she lay comatose. Then, slowly, she came back to life.

First, her pupils started to react to light. Next, she began to breathe on her own. And, one day, she simply awoke. Two weeks after her accident, she went home. Her right leg and left arm were partially paralyzed. Her speech was thick and slurry. But she underwent extensive outpatient therapy. By age five, she had recovered her faculties completely. Physical and neurological examinations were normal. She was like any little girl again.

What makes this recovery astounding isn't just the idea that someone could be brought back after two hours in a state that would once have been considered death. It's also the idea that a group of people in a random hospital could manage to pull off something so enormously complicated. Rescuing a drowning victim is nothing like it looks on television shows, where a few chest compressions and some mouth-to-mouth resuscitation always seem to bring someone with waterlogged lungs and a stilled heart coughing and sputtering back to life. To save this one child, scores of people had to carry out thousands of steps correctly: placing the heart-pump tubing into her without letting in air bubbles; maintaining the sterility of her lines, her open chest, the exposed fluid in her brain; keeping a temperamental battery of machines up and running. The degree of difficulty in any one of these steps is substantial. Then you must add the difficulties of orchestrating them in the right sequence, with nothing dropped, leaving some room for improvisation, but not too much.

For every drowned and pulseless child rescued, there are scores more who don't make it—and not just because their bodies are too far gone. Machines break down; a team can't get moving fast enough; someone fails to wash his hands and an infection takes hold. Such cases don't get written up in the *Annals of Thoracic Surgery*, but they are the norm, though people may not realize it.

I think we have been fooled about what we can expect from medicine—fooled, one could say, by penicillin. Alexander Fleming's 1928 discovery held out a beguiling vision of health care and how it would treat illness or injury in the future: a simple pill or injection would be capable of curing not just one condition but perhaps many. Penicillin, after all, seemed to be effective against an astonishing variety of previously untreatable infectious diseases. So why not a similar cure-all for the different kinds of cancer? And why not something equally simple to melt away skin burns or to reverse cardiovascular disease and strokes?

Medicine didn't turn out this way, though. After a century of incredible discovery, most diseases have proved to be far more particular and difficult to treat. This is true even for the infections doctors once treated with penicillin: not all bacterial strains were susceptible and those that were soon developed resistance. Infections today require highly individualized treatment, sometimes with multiple therapies, based on a given strain's pattern of antibiotic susceptibility, the condition of the patient, and which organ systems are affected. The model of medicine in the modern age seems less and less like penicillin and more and more like what was required for the girl who nearly drowned. Medicine has become the art of managing extreme complexity—and a test of whether such complexity can, in fact, be humanly mastered.

The ninth edition of the World Health Organization's international classification of diseases has grown to distinguish more than thirteen thousand different diseases, syndromes, and types of injury—more than thirteen thousand different ways, in other words, that the body can fail. And, for nearly all of them, science has given us things we can do to help. If we cannot cure the disease, then we can usually reduce the harm and misery it causes. But for each condition the steps are different and they are almost never simple. Clinicians now have at their disposal some six thousand drugs and four thousand medical and surgical procedures, each with different requirements, risks, and considerations. It is a lot to get right.

There is a community clinic in Boston's Kenmore Square affiliated with my hospital. The word *clinic* makes the place sound tiny, but it's nothing of the sort. Founded in 1969, and now called Harvard Vanguard, it aimed to provide people with the full range of outpatient medical services they might need over the course of their lives. It has since tried to stick with that plan, but doing so hasn't been easy. To keep up with the explosive growth in medical capabilities, the clinic has had to build more than twenty facilities and employ some six hundred doctors and a thousand other health professionals covering fifty-nine specialties, many of which did not exist when the clinic first opened. Walking the fifty steps from the fifth-floor elevator to the general surgery department, I pass offices for general internal medicine, endocrinology, genetics, hand surgery, laboratory testing, nephrology, ophthalmology, orthopedics, radiology scheduling, and urology—and that's just one hallway.

To handle the complexity, we've split up the tasks among various specialties. But even divvied up, the work can become overwhelming. In the course of one day on general surgery call at the hospital, for instance, the labor floor asked me to see a twenty-five-year-old woman with mounting right lower abdominal pain, fever, and nausea, which raised concern about appendicitis, but she was pregnant, so getting a CT scan to rule out the possibility posed a risk to the fetus. A gynecological oncologist paged me to the operating room about a woman with an ovarian mass that upon removal appeared to be a metastasis from pancreatic cancer; my colleague wanted me to examine her pancreas and decide whether to biopsy it. A physician at a nearby hospital phoned me to transfer a patient in intensive care with a large cancer that had grown to obstruct her kidneys and bowel and produce bleeding that they were having trouble controlling. Our internal medicine service called me to see a sixty-one-year-old man with emphysema so severe he had been refused hip surgery because of insufficient lung reserves; now he had a severe colon infection—an acute diverticulitis—that had worsened despite three days of antibiotics, and surgery seemed his only option. Another service asked for help with a fifty-two-year-old man with diabetes, coronary artery disease, high blood pressure, chronic kidney failure, severe obesity, a stroke, and now a strangulating groin hernia. And an internist called about a young, otherwise healthy woman with a possible rectal abscess to be lanced.

Confronted with cases of such variety and intricacy—in one day, I'd had six patients with six completely different primary medical problems and a total of twenty-six different additional diagnoses—it's tempting to believe that no one else's job could be as complex as mine. But extreme complexity is the rule for almost everyone. I asked the people in Harvard Vanguard's medical records department if they would query the electronic system for how many different kinds of patient problems the average doctor there sees annually. The answer that came back flabbergasted me. Over the course of a year of office practice—which, by definition, excludes the patients seen in the hospital—physicians each evaluated an average of 250 different primary diseases and conditions. Their patients had more than nine hundred other active medical problems that had to be taken into account. The doctors each prescribed some three hundred medications, ordered more than a hundred different types of laboratory tests, and performed an average of forty different kinds of office procedures—from vaccinations to setting fractures.

Even considering just the office work, the statistics still didn't catch all the diseases and conditions. One of the most common diagnoses, it turned out, was "Other." On a hectic day, when you're running two hours behind and the people in the waiting room are getting irate, you may not take the time to record the precise diagnostic codes in the database. But, even when you do have the time, you commonly find that the particular diseases your patients have do not actually exist in the computer system.

The software used in most American electronic records has not managed to include all the diseases that have been discovered and distinguished from one another in recent years. I once saw a patient with a ganglioneuroblastoma (a rare type of tumor of the adrenal gland) and another with a nightmarish genetic condition called Li-Fraumeni syndrome, which causes inheritors to develop cancers in organs all over their bodies. Neither disease had yet made it into the pull-down menus. All I could record was, in so many words, "Other." Scientists continue to report important new genetic findings, subtypes of cancer, and other diagnoses—not to mention treatments—almost weekly. The complexity is increasing so fast that even the computers cannot keep up.

But it's not only the breadth and quantity of knowledge that has made medicine complicated. It is also the execution—the practical matter of what knowledge requires clinicians to do. The hospital is where you see just how formidable the task can be. A prime example is the place the girl who nearly drowned spent most of her recovery—the intensive care unit.

It's an opaque term, *intensive care*. Specialists in the field prefer to call what they do *critical care*, but that still doesn't exactly clarify matters. The nonmedical term *life support* gets us closer. The damage that the human body can survive these days is as awesome as it is horrible: crushing, burning, bombing, a burst aorta, a ruptured colon, a massive heart attack, rampaging infection. These maladies were once uniformly fatal. Now survival is commonplace, and a substantial part of the credit goes to the abilities intensive care units have developed to take artificial control of failing bodies. Typically, this requires a panoply of technology—a mechanical ventilator and perhaps a tracheostomy tube if the lungs have failed, an aortic balloon pump if the heart has given out, a dialysis machine if the kidneys don't work. If you are unconscious and can't eat, silicone tubing can be surgically inserted into your stomach or intestines for formula feeding. If your intestines are too damaged, solutions of amino acids, fatty acids, and glucose can be infused directly into your bloodstream.

On any given day in the United States alone, some ninety thousand people are admitted to intensive care. Over a year, an estimated five million Americans will be, and over a normal lifetime nearly all of us will come to know the glassed bay of an ICU from the inside. Wide swaths of medicine now depend on the life support systems that ICUs provide: care for premature infants; for victims of trauma, strokes, and heart attacks; for patients who have had surgery on their brains, hearts, lungs, or major blood vessels. Critical care has become an increasingly large portion of what hospitals do. Fifty years ago, ICUs barely existed. Now, to take a recent random day in my hospital, 155 of our almost 700 patients are in intensive care. The average stay of an ICU patient is four days, and the survival rate is 86 percent. Going into an ICU, being put on a mechanical ventilator, having tubes and wires run into and out of you, is not a sentence of death. But the days will be the most precarious of your life.

Fifteen years ago, Israeli scientists published a study in which engineers observed patient care in ICUs for twenty-four-hour stretches. They found that the average patient required 178 individual actions per day, ranging from administering a drug to suctioning the lungs, and every one of them posed risks. Remarkably, the nurses and doctors were observed to make an error in just 1 percent of these actions—but that still amounted to an average of two errors a day with every patient. Intensive care succeeds only when we hold the odds of doing harm low enough for the odds of doing good to prevail. This is hard. There are dangers simply in lying unconscious in bed for a few days. Muscles atrophy. Bones lose mass. Pressure ulcers form. Veins begin to clot. You have to stretch and exercise patients' flaccid limbs daily to avoid contractures; you have to give subcutaneous injections of blood thinners at least twice a day, turn patients in bed every few hours, bathe them and change their sheets without knocking out a tube or a line, brush their teeth twice a day to avoid pneumonia from bacterial buildup in their mouths. Add a ventilator, dialysis, and the care of open wounds, and the difficulties only accumulate.

The story of one of my patients makes the point. Anthony DeFilippo was a forty-eight-year-old limousine driver from Everett, Massachusetts, who started to hemorrhage at a community hospital during surgery for a hernia and gallstones. The surgeon was finally able to stop the bleeding but DeFilippo's liver was severely damaged, and over the next few days he became too sick for the hospital's facilities. I accepted him for transfer in order to stabilize him and figure out what to do. When he arrived in our ICU, at 1:30 a.m. on a Sunday, his ragged black hair was plastered to his sweaty forehead, his body was shaking, and his heart was racing at 114 beats a minute. He was delirious from fever, shock, and low oxygen levels.

"I need to get out!" he cried. "I need to get out!" He clawed at his gown, his oxygen mask, the dressings covering his abdominal wound.

"Tony, it's all right," a nurse said to him. "We're going to help you. You're in a hospital."

He shoved her out of the way—he was a big man—and tried to swing his legs out of the bed. We turned up his oxygen flow, put his wrists in cloth restraints, and tried to reason with him. He eventually tired out and let us draw blood and give him antibiotics.

The laboratory results came back showing liver failure and a steeply elevated white blood cell count, indicating infection. It soon became evident from his empty urine bag that his kidneys had failed, too. In the next few hours, his blood pressure fell, his breathing worsened, and he drifted from agitation to near unconsciousness. Each of his organ systems, including his brain, was shutting down.

I called his sister, his next of kin, and told her the situation. "Do everything you can," she said.

So we did. We gave him a syringeful of anesthetic, and a resident slid a breathing tube into his throat. Another resident "lined him up." She inserted a thin two-inch-long needle and catheter through his upturned right wrist and into his radial artery, then sewed the line to his skin with a silk suture. Next, she put in a central line—a twelve-inch catheter pushed into the jugular vein in his left neck. After she sewed that in place, and an X-ray showed its tip floating just where it was supposed to—inside his vena cava at the entrance to his heart—she put a third, slightly thicker line, for dialysis, through his right upper chest and into the subclavian vein, deep under the collarbone.

We hooked a breathing tube up to a hose from a ventilator and set it to give him fourteen forced breaths of 100 percent oxygen every minute. We dialed the ventilator pressures and gas flow up and down, like engineers at a control panel, until we got the blood levels of oxygen and carbon dioxide where we wanted them. The arterial line gave us continuous arterial blood pressure measurements, and we tweaked his medications to get the pressures we liked. We regulated his intravenous fluids according to venous pressure measurements from his jugular line. We plugged his subclavian line into tubing from a dialysis machine, and every few minutes his entire blood volume washed through this artificial kidney and back into his body; a little adjustment here and there, and we could alter the levels of potassium and bicarbonate and salt, as well. He was, we liked to imagine, a simple machine in our hands.

But he wasn't, of course. It was as if we had gained a steering wheel and a few gauges and controls, but on a runaway 18-wheeler hurtling down a mountain. Keeping that patient's blood pressure normal required gallons of intravenous fluid and a pharmacy shelf of drugs. He was on near-maximal ventilator support. His temperature climbed to 104 degrees. Less than 5 percent of patients with DeFilippo's degree of organ failure make it home. A single misstep could easily erase those slender chances.

For ten days, though, we made progress. DeFilippo's chief problem had been liver damage from his prior operation: the main duct from his liver was severed and was leaking bile, which is caustic—it digests the fat in one's diet and was essentially eating him alive from the inside. He had become too sick to survive an operation to repair the leak. So once we had stabilized him, we tried a temporary solution—we had radiologists place a plastic drain, using CT guidance, through his abdominal wall and into the severed duct in order to draw out the leaking bile. They found so much that they had to place three drains—one inside the duct and two around it. But, as the bile drained out, his fevers subsided. His need for oxygen and fluids diminished, and his blood pressure returned to normal. He was beginning to mend. Then, on the eleventh day, just as we were getting ready to take him off the ventilator, he again developed high, spiking fevers, his blood pressure sank, and his blood-oxygen levels plummeted again. His skin became clammy. He got shaking chills.

We couldn't understand what had happened. He seemed to have developed an infection, but our X-rays and CT scans failed to turn up a source. Even after we put him on four antibiotics, he continued to spike fevers. During one fever, his heart went into fibrillation. A Code Blue was called. A dozen nurses and doctors raced to his bedside, slapped electric paddles onto his chest, and shocked him. His heart responded and went back into rhythm. It took two more days for us to figure out what had gone wrong. We considered the possibility that one of his lines had become infected, so we put in new lines and sent the old ones to the lab for culturing. Forty-eight hours later, the results returned. All the lines were infected. The infection had probably started in one line, which perhaps was contaminated during insertion, and spread through DeFilippo's bloodstream to the others. Then they all began spilling bacteria into him, producing the fevers and steep decline.

This is the reality of intensive care: at any point, we are as apt to harm as we are to heal. Line infections are so common that they are considered a routine complication. ICUs put five million lines into patients each year, and national statistics show that after ten days 4 percent of those lines become infected. Line infections occur in eighty thousand people a year in the United States and are fatal between 5 and 28 percent of the time, depending on how sick one is at the start. Those who survive line infections spend on average a week longer in intensive care. And this is just one of many risks. After ten days with a urinary catheter, 4 percent of American ICU patients develop a bladder infection. After ten days on a ventilator, 6 percent develop bacterial pneumonia, resulting in death 40 to 45 percent of the time. All in all, about half of ICU patients end up experiencing a serious complication, and once that occurs the chances of survival drop sharply.

It was another week before DeFilippo recovered sufficiently from his infections to come off the ventilator and two months before he left the hospital. Weak and debilitated, he lost his limousine business and his home, and he had to move in with his sister. The tube draining bile still dangled from his abdomen; when he was stronger, I was going to have to do surgery to reconstruct the main bile duct from his liver. But he survived. Most people in his situation do not.

Here, then, is the fundamental puzzle of modern medical care: you have a desperately sick patient and in order to have a chance of saving him you have to get the knowledge right and then you have to make sure that the 178 daily tasks that follow are done correctly—despite some monitor's alarm going off for God knows what reason, despite the patient in the next bed crashing, despite a nurse poking his head around the curtain to ask whether someone could help "get this lady's chest open." There is complexity upon complexity. And even specialization has begun to seem inadequate. So what do you do?

The medical profession's answer has been to go from specialization to superspecialization. I told DeFilippo's ICU story, for instance, as if I were the one tending to him hour by hour. That, however, was actually an intensivist (as intensive care specialists like to be called). As a general surgeon, I like to think I can handle most clinical situations. But, as the intricacies involved in intensive care have grown, responsibility has increasingly shifted to superspecialists. In the past decade, training programs focusing on critical care have opened in most major American and European cities, and half of American ICUs now rely on superspecialists.

Expertise is the mantra of modern medicine. In the early twentieth century, you needed only a high school diploma and a one-year medical degree to practice medicine. By the century's end, all doctors had to have a college degree, a four-year medical degree, and an additional three to seven years of residency training in an individual field of practice—pediatrics, surgery, neurology, or the like. In recent years, though, even this level of preparation has not been enough for the new complexity of medicine. After their residencies, most young doctors today are going on to do fellowships, adding one to three further years of training in, say, laparoscopic surgery, or pediatric metabolic disorders, or breast radiology, or critical care. A young doctor is not so young nowadays; you typically don't start in independent practice until your midthirties.

We live in the era of the superspecialist—of clinicians who have taken the time to practice, practice, practice at one narrow thing until they can do it better than anyone else. They have two advantages over ordinary specialists: greater knowledge of the details that matter and a learned ability to handle the complexities of the particular job. There are degrees of complexity, though, and medicine and other fields like it have grown so far beyond the usual kind that avoiding daily mistakes is proving impossible even for our most superspecialized.

There is perhaps no field that has taken specialization further than surgery. Think of the operating room as a particularly aggressive intensive care unit. We have anesthesiologists just to handle pain control and patient stability, and even they have divided into subcategories. There are pediatric anesthesiologists, cardiac anesthesiologists, obstetric anesthesiologists, neurosurgical anesthesiologists, and many others. Likewise, we no longer have just "operating room nurses." They too are often subspecialized for specific kinds of cases.

Then of course there are the surgeons. Surgeons are so absurdly ultraspecialized that when we joke about right ear surgeons and left ear surgeons, we have to check to be sure they don't exist. I am trained as a general surgeon but, except in the most rural places, there is no such thing. You really can't do everything anymore. I decided to center my practice on surgical oncology—cancer surgery—but even this proved too broad. So, although I have done all I can to hang on to a broad span of general surgical skills, especially for emergencies, I've developed a particular expertise in removing cancers of endocrine glands.

The result of the recent decades of ever-refined specialization has been a spectacular improvement in surgical capability and success. Where deaths were once a double-digit risk of even small operations, and prolonged recovery and disability was the norm, day surgery has become commonplace.

Yet given how much surgery is now done—Americans today undergo an average of seven operations in their lifetime, with surgeons performing more than fifty million operations annually—the amount of harm remains substantial. We continue to have upwards of 150,000 deaths following surgery every year—more than three times the number of road traffic fatalities. Moreover, research has consistently showed that at least half our deaths and major complications are avoidable. The knowledge exists. But however supremely specialized and trained we may have become, steps are still missed. Mistakes are still made.

Medicine, with its dazzling successes but also frequent failures, therefore poses a significant challenge: What do you do when expertise is not enough? What do you do when even the super-specialists fail? We've begun to see an answer, but it has come from an unexpected source—one that has nothing to do with medicine at all.

2. THE CHECKLIST

at Wright Air Field in Dayton, Ohio, the U.S. Army Air Corps held a flight competition for airplane manufacturers vying to build the military's next-generation long-range bomber. It wasn't supposed to be much of a competition. In early evaluations, the Boeing Corporation's gleaming aluminum-alloy Model 299 had trounced the designs of Martin and Douglas. Boeing's plane could carry five times as many bombs as the army had requested; it could fly faster than previous bombers and almost twice as far. A Seattle newspaperman who had glimpsed the plane on a test flight over his city called it the "flying fortress," and the name stuck. The flight "competition," according to the military historian Phillip Meilinger, was regarded as a mere formality. The army planned to order at least sixty-five of the aircraft.

A small crowd of army brass and manufacturing executives watched as the Model 299 test plane taxied onto the runway. It was sleek and impressive, with a 103-foot wingspan and four engines jutting out from the wings, rather than the usual two. The plane roared down the tarmac, lifted off smoothly, and climbed sharply to three hundred feet. Then it stalled, turned on one wing, and crashed in a fiery explosion. Two of the five crew members died, including the pilot, Major Ployer P. Hill.

An investigation revealed that nothing mechanical had gone wrong. The crash had been due to "pilot error," the report said. Substantially more complex than previous aircraft, the new plane required the pilot to attend to the four engines, each with its own oil-fuel mix, the retractable landing gear, the wing flaps, electric trim tabs that needed adjustment to maintain stability at different airspeeds, and constant-speed propellers whose pitch had to be regulated with hydraulic controls, among other features. While doing all this, Hill had forgotten to release a new locking mechanism on the elevator and rudder controls. The Boeing model was deemed, as a newspaper put it, "too much airplane for one man to fly." The army air corps declared Douglas's smaller design the winner. Boeing nearly went bankrupt.

Still, the army purchased a few aircraft from Boeing as test planes, and some insiders remained convinced that the aircraft was flyable. So a group of test pilots got together and considered what to do.

What they decided *not* to do was almost as interesting as what they actually did. They did not require Model 299 pilots to undergo longer training. It was hard to imagine having more experience and expertise than Major Hill, who had been the air corps' chief of flight testing. Instead, they came up with an ingeniously

simple approach: they created a pilot's checklist. Its mere exis-
tence indicated how far aeronautics had advanced. In the early
years of flight, getting an aircraft into the air might have been
nerve-racking but it was hardly complex. Using a checklist for
takeoff would no more have occurred to a pilot than to a driver
backing a car out of the garage. But flying this new plane was too
complicated to be left to the memory of any one person, however expert.

The test pilots made their list simple, brief, and to the point—
short enough to fit on an index card, with step-by-step checks for
takeoff, flight, landing, and taxiing. It had the kind of stuff that
all pilots know to do. They check that the brakes are released,
that the instruments are set, that the door and windows are
closed, that the elevator controls are unlocked—dumb stuff. You
wouldn't think it would make that much difference. But with the
checklist in hand, the pilots went on to fly the Model 299 a total
of 1.8 million miles without one accident. The army ultimately
ordered almost thirteen thousand of the aircraft, which it dubbed
the B-17. And, because flying the behemoth was now possible,
the army gained a decisive air advantage in the Second World
War, enabling its devastating bombing campaign across Nazi
Germany.

Much of our work today has entered its own B-17 phase. Substantial parts of what software designers, financial managers, firefighters, police officers, lawyers, and most certainly clinicians do
are now too complex for them to carry out reliably from memory alone. Multiple fields, in other words, have become too much
airplane for one person to fly.

Yet it is far from obvious that something as simple as a checklist
could be of substantial help. We may admit that errors and over-

sights occur—even devastating ones. But we believe our jobs are too complicated to reduce to a checklist. Sick people, for instance, are phenomenally more various than airplanes. A study of forty-one thousand trauma patients in the state of Pennsylvania—just trauma patients—found that they had 1,224 different injury-related diagnoses in 32,261 unique combinations. That's like having 32,261 kinds of airplane to land. Mapping out the proper steps for every case is not possible, and physicians have been skeptical that a piece of paper with a bunch of little boxes would improve matters.

But we have had glimmers that it might, at least in some corners. What, for instance, are the vital signs that every hospital records if not a kind of checklist? Comprised of four physiological data points—body temperature, pulse, blood pressure, and respiratory rate—they give health professionals a basic picture of how sick a person is. Missing one of these measures can be dangerous, we've learned. Maybe three of them seem normal—the patient looks good, actually—and you're inclined to say, "Eh, she's fine, send her home." But perhaps the fourth reveals a fever or low blood pressure or a galloping heart rate, and skipping it could cost a person her life.

Practitioners have had the means to measure vital signs since the early twentieth century, after the mercury thermometer became commonplace and the Russian physician Nicolai Korotkoff demonstrated how to use an inflatable sleeve and stethoscope to quantify blood pressure. But although using the four signs together as a group gauged the condition of patients more accurately than using any of them singly, clinicians did not reliably record them all.

In a complex environment, experts are up against two main

difficulties. The first is the fallibility of human memory and attention, especially when it comes to mundane, routine matters that are easily overlooked under the strain of more pressing events. (When you've got a patient throwing up and an upset family member asking you what's going on, it can be easy to forget that you have not checked her pulse.) Faulty memory and distraction are a particular danger in what engineers call all-or-none processes: whether running to the store to buy ingredients for a cake, preparing an airplane for takeoff, or evaluating a sick person in the hospital, if you miss just one key thing, you might as well not have made the effort at all.

A further difficulty, just as insidious, is that people can lull themselves into skipping steps even when they remember them. In complex processes, after all, certain steps don't *always* matter. Perhaps the elevator controls on airplanes are usually unlocked and a check is pointless most of the time. Perhaps measuring all four vital signs uncovers a worrisome issue in only one out of fifty patients. "This has never been a problem before," people say. Until one day it is.

Checklists seem to provide protection against such failures. They remind us of the minimum necessary steps and make them explicit. They not only offer the possibility of verification but also instill a kind of discipline of higher performance. Which is precisely what happened with vital signs—though it was not doctors who deserved the credit.

The routine recording of the four vital signs did not become the norm in Western hospitals until the 1960s, when nurses embraced the idea. They designed their patient charts and forms to include the signs, essentially creating a checklist for themselves.

With all the things nurses had to do for their patients over the course of a day or night—dispense their medications, dress their wounds, troubleshoot problems—the "vitals chart" provided a way of ensuring that every six hours, or more often when nurses judged necessary, they didn't forget to check their patient's pulse, blood pressure, temperature, and respiration and assess exactly how the patient was doing.

In most hospitals, nurses have since added a fifth vital sign: pain, as rated by patients on a scale of one to ten. And nurses have developed yet further such bedside innovations—for example, medication timing charts and brief written care plans for every patient. No one calls these checklists but, really, that's what they are. They have been welcomed by nursing but haven't quite carried over into doctoring.

Charts and checklists, that's nursing stuff—boring stuff. They are nothing that we doctors, with our extra years of training and specialization, would ever need or use.

In 2001, though, a critical care specialist at Johns Hopkins Hospital named Peter Pronovost decided to give a doctor checklist a try. He didn't attempt to make the checklist encompass everything ICU teams might need to do in a day. He designed it to tackle just one of their hundreds of potential tasks, the one that nearly killed Anthony DeFilippo: central line infections.

On a sheet of plain paper, he plotted out the steps to take in order to avoid infections when putting in a central line. Doctors are supposed to (1) wash their hands with soap, (2) clean the patient's skin with chlorhexidine antiseptic, (3) put sterile drapes over the entire patient, (4) wear a mask, hat, sterile gown, and gloves, and (5) put a sterile dressing over the insertion site once the line is in. Check, check, check, check, check. These steps are no-brainers; they have been known and taught for years. So it seemed silly to make a checklist for something so obvious. Still, Pronovost asked the nurses in his ICU to observe the doctors for a month as they put lines into patients and record how often they carried out each step. In more than a third of patients, they skipped at least one.

The next month, he and his team persuaded the Johns Hopkins Hospital administration to authorize nurses to stop doctors if they saw them skipping a step on the checklist; nurses were also to ask the doctors each day whether any lines ought to be removed, so as not to leave them in longer than necessary. This was revolutionary. Nurses have always had their ways of nudging a doctor into doing the right thing, ranging from the gentle reminder ("Um, did you forget to put on your mask, doctor?") to more forceful methods (I've had a nurse bodycheck me when she thought I hadn't put enough drapes on a patient). But many nurses aren't sure whether this is their place or whether a given measure is worth a confrontation. (Does it really matter whether a patient's legs are draped for a line going into the chest?) The new rule made it clear: if doctors didn't follow every step, the nurses would have backup from the administration to intervene.

For a year afterward, Pronovost and his colleagues monitored what happened. The results were so dramatic that they weren't sure whether to believe them: the ten-day line-infection rate went from 11 percent to zero. So they followed patients for fifteen more months. Only two line infections occurred during the entire period. They calculated that, in this one hospital, the checklist had prevented forty-three infections and eight deaths and saved two million dollars in costs.

Pronovost recruited more colleagues, and they tested some more checklists in his Johns Hopkins ICU. One aimed to ensure that nurses observed patients for pain at least once every four hours and provided timely pain medication. This reduced from 41 percent to 3 percent the likelihood of a patient's enduring untreated pain. They tested a checklist for patients on mechanical ventilation, making sure, for instance, that doctors prescribed antacid medication to prevent stomach ulcers and that the head of each patient's bed was propped up at least thirty degrees to stop oral secretions from going into the windpipe. The proportion of patients not receiving the recommended care dropped from 70 percent to 4 percent, the occurrence of pneumonias fell by a quarter, and twenty-one fewer patients died than in the previous year. The researchers found that simply having the doctors and nurses in the ICU create their own checklists for what they thought should be done each day improved the consistency of care to the point that the average length of patient stay in intensive care dropped by half.

These checklists accomplished what checklists elsewhere have done, Pronovost observed. They helped with memory recall and clearly set out the minimum necessary steps in a process. He was surprised to discover how often even experienced personnel failed to grasp the importance of certain precautions. In a survey of ICU staff taken before introducing the ventilator checklists, he found that half hadn't realized that evidence strongly supported giving ventilated patients antacid medication. Checklists, he found, established a higher standard of baseline performance.

These seem, of course, ridiculously primitive insights.

Pronovost is routinely described by colleagues as "brilliant," "inspiring," a "genius." He has an M.D. and a Ph.D. in public health from Johns Hopkins and is trained in emergency medicine, anesthesiology, and critical care medicine. But, really, does it take all that to figure out what anyone who has made a to-do list figured out ages ago? Well, maybe yes.

Despite his initial checklist results, takers were slow to come. He traveled around the country showing his checklists to doctors, nurses, insurers, employers—anyone who would listen. He spoke in an average of seven cities a month. But few adopted the idea.

There were various reasons. Some physicians were offended by the suggestion that they needed checklists. Others had legitimate doubts about Pronovost's evidence. So far, he'd shown only that checklists worked in one hospital, Johns Hopkins, where the ICUs have money, plenty of staff, and Peter Pronovost walking the hallways to make sure that the idea was being properly implemented. How about in the real world—where ICU nurses and doctors are in short supply, pressed for time, overwhelmed with patients, and hardly receptive to the notion of filling out yet another piece of paper?

In 2003, however, the Michigan Health and Hospital Association approached Pronovost about testing his central line checklist throughout the state's ICUs. It would be a huge undertaking. But Pronovost would have a chance to establish whether his checklists could really work in the wider world.

I visited Sinai-Grace Hospital, in inner-city Detroit, a few years after the project was under way, and I saw what Pronovost was up against. Occupying a campus of redbrick buildings amid abandoned houses, check-cashing stores, and wig shops on the city's West Side, just south of Eight Mile Road, Sinai-Grace is a classic urban hospital. It employed at the time eight hundred physicians, seven hundred nurses, and two thousand other medical personnel to care for a population with the lowest median income of any city in the country. More than a quarter of a million residents were uninsured; 300,000 were on state assistance. That meant chronic financial problems. Sinai-Grace is not the most cash-strapped hospital in the city—that would be Detroit Receiving Hospital, where more than a fifth of the patients have no means of payment. But between 2000 and 2003, Sinai-Grace and eight other Detroit hospitals were forced to cut a third of their staff, and the state had to come forward with a $50 million bailout to avert their bankruptcy.

Sinai-Grace has five ICUs for adult patients and one for infants. Hassan Makki, the director of intensive care, told me what it was like there in 2004, when Pronovost and the hospital association started a series of mailings and conference calls with hospitals to introduce checklists for central lines and ventilator patients. "Morale was low," he said. "We had lost lots of staff, and the nurses who remained weren't sure if they were staying." Many doctors were thinking about leaving, too. Meanwhile, the teams faced an even heavier workload because of new rules limiting how long the residents could work at a stretch. Now Pronovost was telling them to find the time to fill out some daily checklists?

Tom Piskorowski, one of the ICU physicians, told me his reaction: "Forget the paperwork. Take care of the patient."

I accompanied a team on 7:00 a.m. rounds through one of the surgical ICUs. It had eleven patients. Four had gunshot wounds (one had been shot in the chest; one had been shot through the bowel, kidney, and liver; two had been shot through the neck and left quadriplegic). Five patients had cerebral hemorrhaging (three were seventy-nine years and older and had been injured falling down stairs; one was a middle-aged man whose skull and left temporal lobe had been damaged by an assault with a blunt weapon; and one was a worker who had become paralyzed from the neck down after falling twenty-five feet off a ladder onto his head). There was a cancer patient recovering from surgery to remove part of his lung, and a patient who had had surgery to repair a cerebral aneurysm.

The doctors and nurses on rounds tried to proceed methodically from one room to the next but were constantly interrupted: a patient they thought they'd stabilized began hemorrhaging again; another who had been taken off the ventilator developed trouble breathing and had to be put back on the machine. It was hard to imagine that they could get their heads far enough above the daily tide of disasters to worry about the minutiae on some checklist.

Yet there they were, I discovered, filling out those pages. Mostly, it was the nurses who kept things in order. Each morning, a senior nurse walked through the unit, clipboard in hand, making sure that every patient on a ventilator had the bed propped at the right angle and had been given the right medicines and the right tests. Whenever doctors put in a central line, a nurse made sure that the central line checklist had been filled out and placed in the patient's chart. Looking back through the hospital files, I found that they had been doing this faithfully for more than three years.

Pronovost had been canny when he started. In his first conversations with hospital administrators, he hadn't ordered them to use the central line checklist. Instead, he asked them simply to gather data on their own line infection rates. In early 2004, they found, the infection rates for ICU patients in Michigan hospitals were higher than the national average, and in some hospitals dramatically so. Sinai-Grace experienced more central line infections than 75 percent of American hospitals. Meanwhile, Blue Cross Blue Shield of Michigan agreed to give hospitals small bonus payments for participating in Pronovost's program. A checklist suddenly seemed an easy and logical thing to try.

In what became known as the Keystone Initiative, each hospital assigned a project manager to roll out the checklist and participate in twice-monthly conference calls with Pronovost for troubleshooting. Pronovost also insisted that the participating hospitals assign to each unit a senior hospital executive who would visit at least once a month, hear the staff's complaints, and help them solve problems.

The executives were reluctant. They normally lived in meetings, worrying about strategy and budgets. They weren't used to venturing into patient territory and didn't feel they belonged there. In some places, they encountered hostility, but their involvement proved crucial. In the first month, the executives discovered that chlorhexidine soap, shown to reduce line infections, was available in less than a third of the ICUs. This was a problem only an executive could solve. Within weeks, every ICU in Michigan had a supply of the soap. Teams also complained to the hospital officials that, although the checklist required patients be fully covered with a sterile drape when lines were being put in, full-size drapes were often unavailable. So the officials made sure that drapes were stocked. Then they persuaded Arrow International, one of the largest manufacturers of central lines, to produce a new kit that had both the drape and chlorhexidine in it.

In December 2006, the Keystone Initiative published its findings in a landmark article in the *New England Journal of Medicine*. Within the first three months of the project, the central line infection rate in Michigan's ICUs decreased by 66 percent. Most ICUs—including the ones at Sinai-Grace Hospital—cut their quarterly infection rate to zero. Michigan's infection rates fell so low that its average ICU outperformed 90 percent of ICUs nationwide. In the Keystone Initiative's first eighteen months, the hospitals saved an estimated $175 million in costs and more than fifteen hundred lives. The successes have been sustained for several years now—all because of a stupid little checklist.

It is tempting to think this might be an isolated success. Perhaps there is something unusual about the strategy required to prevent central line infections. After all, the central line checklist did not prevent any of the other kinds of complications that can result from sticking these foot-long plastic catheters into people's chests—such as a collapsed lung if the needle goes in too deep or bleeding if a blood vessel gets torn. It just prevented infections. In this particular instance, yes, doctors had some trouble getting the basics right—making sure to wash their hands, put on their sterile gloves and gown, and so on—and a checklist proved dramatically valuable. But among the myriad tasks clinicians carry out for patients, maybe this is the peculiar case.

I started to wonder, though.

Around the time I learned of Pronovost's results, I spoke to Markus Thalmann, the cardiac surgeon who had been the lead author of the case report on the extraordinary rescue of the little girl from death by drowning. Among the many details that intrigued me about the save was the fact that it occurred not at a large cutting-edge academic medical center but at an ordinary community hospital. This one was in Klagenfurt, a small provincial Austrian town in the Alps nearest to where the girl had fallen in the pond. I asked Thalmann how the hospital had managed such a complicated rescue.

He told me he had been working in Klagenfurt for six years when the girl came in. She had not been the first person whom he and his colleagues had tried to revive from cardiac arrest after hypothermia and suffocation. His hospital received between three and five such patients a year, he estimated, mostly avalanche victims, some of them drowning victims, and a few of them people attempting suicide by taking a drug overdose and then wandering out into the snowy Alpine forests to fall unconscious. For a long time, he said, no matter how hard the hospital's medical staff tried, they had no survivors. Most of the victims had been without a pulse and oxygen for too long when they were found. But some, he was convinced, still had a flicker of viability in them, yet he and his colleagues had always failed to sustain it.

He took a close look at the case records. Preparation, he determined, was the chief difficulty. Success required having an array of people and equipment at the ready—trauma surgeons, a cardiac anesthesiologist, a cardiothoracic surgeon, bioengineering support staff, a cardiac perfusionist, operating and critical care nurses, intensivists. Almost routinely, someone or something was missing.

He tried the usual surgical approach to remedy this—yelling at everyone to get their act together. But still they had no saves.

So he and a couple of colleagues decided to try something new. They made a checklist.

They gave the checklist to the people with the least power in the whole process—the rescue squads and the hospital telephone operator—and walked them through the details. In cases like these, the checklist said, rescue teams were to tell the hospital to prepare for possible cardiac bypass and rewarming. They were to call, when possible, even before they arrived on the scene, as the preparation time could be significant. The telephone operator would then work down a list of people to notify them to have everything set up and standing by.

With the checklist in place, the team had its first success—the rescue of the three-year-old girl. Not long afterward, Thalmann left to take a job at a hospital in Vienna. The team, however, has since had at least two other such rescues, he said. In one case, a man had been found frozen and pulseless after a suicide attempt. In another, a mother and her sixteen-year-old daughter were in an accident that sent them and their car through a guardrail, over a cliff, and into a mountain river. The mother died on impact; the daughter was trapped as the car rapidly filled with icy water. She had been in cardiac and respiratory arrest for a prolonged period of time when the rescue team arrived.

From that point onward, though, everything moved like clockwork. By the time the rescue team got to her and began CPR, the hospital had been notified. The transport team delivered her in minutes. The surgical team took her straight to the operating room and crashed her onto heart-lung bypass. One step followed right after another. And, because of the speed with which they did, she had a chance.

As the girl's body slowly rewarmed, her heart came back. In the ICU, a mechanical ventilator, fluids, and intravenous drugs kept her going while the rest of her body recovered. The next day, the doctors were able to remove her lines and tubes. The day after that, she was sitting up in bed, ready to go home.

3. THE END OF THE MASTER BUILDER

Four generations after the first aviation checklists went into use, a lesson is emerging: checklists seem able to defend anyone, even the experienced, against failure in many more tasks than we realized. They provide a kind of cognitive net. They catch mental flaws inherent in all of us—flaws of memory and attention and thoroughness. And because they do, they raise wide, unexpected possibilities.

But they presumably have limits, as well. So a key step is to identify which kinds of situations checklists can help with and which ones they can't.

Two professors who study the science of complexity—Brenda Zimmerman of York University and Sholom Glouberman of the University of Toronto—have proposed a distinction among three different kinds of problems in the world: the simple, the complicated, and the complex. Simple problems, they note, are ones like baking a cake from a mix. There is a recipe. Sometimes there are a few basic techniques to learn. But once these are mastered, following the recipe brings a high likelihood of success.

Complicated problems are ones like sending a rocket to the moon. They can sometimes be broken down into a series of simple problems. But there is no straightforward recipe. Success frequently requires multiple people, often multiple teams, and specialized expertise. Unanticipated difficulties are frequent. Timing and coordination become serious concerns.

Complex problems are ones like raising a child. Once you learn how to send a rocket to the moon, you can repeat the process with other rockets and perfect it. One rocket is like another rocket. But not so with raising a child, the professors point out. Every child is unique. Although raising one child may provide experience, it does not guarantee success with the next child. Expertise is valuable but most certainly not sufficient. Indeed, the next child may require an entirely different approach from the previous one. And this brings up another feature of complex problems: their outcomes remain highly uncertain. Yet we all know that it is possible to raise a child well. It's complex, that's all.

Thinking about averting plane crashes in 1935, or stopping infections of central lines in 2003, or rescuing drowning victims today, I realized that the key problem in each instance was essentially a simple one, despite the number of contributing factors. One needed only to focus attention on the rudder and elevator controls in the first case, to maintain sterility in the second, and to be prepared for cardiac bypass in the third. All were amenable, as a result, to what engineers call "forcing functions": relatively straightforward solutions that force the necessary behavior—solutions like checklists.

We are besieged by simple problems. In medicine, these are the failures to don a mask when putting in a central line or to recall that one of the ten causes of a flat-line cardiac arrest is a potassium overdose. In legal practice, these are the failures to remember all the critical avenues of defense in a tax fraud case or simply the various court deadlines. In police work, these are the failures to conduct an eyewitness lineup properly, forgetting to tell the witness that the perpetrator of the crime may not be in the lineup, for instance, or having someone present who knows which one the suspect is. Checklists can provide protection against such elementary errors.

Much of the most critical work people do, however, is not so simple. Putting in a central line is just one of the 178 tasks an ICU team must coordinate and execute in a day—ICU work is complicated—and are we really going to be able to create and follow checklists for every possible one of them? Is this even remotely practical? There is no straightforward recipe for the care of ICU patients. It requires multiple practitioners orchestrating different combinations of tasks for different conditions—matters that cannot be controlled by simple forcing functions.

Plus, people are individual in ways that rockets are not—they are complex. No two pneumonia patients are identical. Even with the same bacteria, the same cough and shortness of breath, the same low oxygen levels, the same antibiotic, one patient might get better and the other might not. A doctor must be prepared for unpredictable turns that checklists seem completely unsuited to address. Medicine contains the entire range of problems—the simple, the complicated, *and* the complex—and there are often times when a clinician has to just do what needs to be done. Forget the paperwork. Take care of the patient.

I have been thinking about these matters for a long time now. I want to be a good doctor for my patients. And the question of when to follow one's judgment and when to follow protocol is central to doing the job well—or to doing anything else that is hard. You want people to make sure to get the stupid stuff right. Yet you also want to leave room for craft and judgment and the ability to respond to unexpected difficulties that arise along the way. The value of checklists for simple problems seems self-evident. But can they help avert failure when the problems combine everything from the simple to the complex?

I happened across an answer in an unlikely place. I found it as I was just strolling down the street one day.

It was a bright January morning in 2007. I was on my way to work, walking along the sidewalk from the parking lot to the main entrance of my hospital, when I came upon a new building under construction for our medical center. It was only a skeleton of steel beams at that point, but it stretched eleven stories high, occupied a full city block, and seemed to have arisen almost overnight from the empty lot that had been there. I stood at one corner watching a construction worker welding a joint as he balanced on a girder four stories above me. And I wondered: How did he and all his co-workers know that they were building this thing right? How could they be sure that it wouldn't fall down?

The building was not unusually large. It would provide 150 private hospital beds (so we could turn our main tower's old, mostly shared rooms into private beds as well) and sixteen fancy new operating rooms (which I was especially looking forward to)—nothing out of the ordinary. I would bet that in the previous year dozens of bigger buildings had been constructed around the country.

Still, this one was no small undertaking, as the hospital's real estate manager later told me. The building, he said, would be 350,000 square feet in size, with three stories underground in addition to the eleven stories above. It would cost $360 million, fully delivered, and require 3,885 tons of steel, thirteen thousand yards of concrete, nineteen air handling units, sixteen elevators, one cooling tower, and one backup emergency generator. The construction workers would have to dig out 100,000 cubic yards of dirt and install 64,000 feet of copper piping, forty-seven miles of conduit, and ninety-five miles of electrical wire—enough to reach Maine.

And, oh yeah, I thought to myself, this thing couldn't fall down.

When I was eleven years old, growing up in Athens, Ohio, I decided I was going to build myself a bookcase. My mother gave me ten dollars, and I biked down to the C&E Hardware store on Richland Avenue. With the help of the nice man with hairy ears behind the counter, I bought four pine planks, each eight inches wide and three-quarters of an inch thick and cut to four feet long. I also bought a tin of stain, a tin of varnish, some sandpaper, and a box of common nails. I lugged the stuff home to our garage. I carefully measured my dimensions. Then I nailed the two cross planks into the two side planks and stood my new bookcase up. It looked perfect. I sanded down the surfaces, applied the stain and soon the varnish. I took it to my bedroom and put a half dozen books on it. Then I watched the whole thing fall sideways like a drunk tipping over. The two middle boards began pulling out. So I hammered in a few more nails and stood the bookcase up again. It tipped over the other way. I banged in some more nails, this time coming in at an angle, thinking that would do the trick. It didn't. Finally, I just nailed the damn thing directly into the wall. And that was how I discovered the concept of bracing.

So as I looked up at this whole building that had to stand up straight even in an earthquake, puzzling over how the workers could be sure they were constructing it properly, I realized the question had two components. First, how could they be sure that they had the right knowledge in hand? Second, how could they be sure that they were applying this knowledge correctly?

Both aspects are tricky. In designing a building, experts must take into account a disconcertingly vast range of factors: the make-up of the local soil, the desired height of the individual structure, the strength of the materials available, and the geometry, to name just a few. Then, to turn the paper plans into reality, they presumably face equally byzantine difficulties making sure that all the different tradesmen and machinery do their job the right way, in the right sequence, while also maintaining the flexibility to adjust for unexpected difficulties and changes.

Yet builders clearly succeed. They safely put up millions of buildings all over the globe. And they do so despite the fact that construction work has grown infinitely more complex over the decades. Moreover, they do it with a frontline workforce that regards each particular job—from pile-driving to wiring intensive care units—much the way doctors, teachers, and other professionals regard their jobs: as specialized domains in which others should not interfere.

I paid a visit to Joe Salvia, the structural engineer for our new hospital wing. I told him I wanted to find out how work is done in his profession. It turned out I'd come to the right person. His firm, McNamara/Salvia, has provided the structural engineering for most of the major hospital buildings in Boston since the late 1960s, and for a considerable percentage of the hotels, office towers, and condominiums as well. It did the structural rebuilding of Fenway Park, the Boston Red Sox baseball team's thirty-six-thousand-seat stadium, including the Green Monster, its iconic thirty-seven-foot, home-run-stealing left field wall. And the firm's particular specialty has been designing and engineering large, complicated, often high-rise structures all over the country.

Salvia's tallest skyscraper is an eighty-story tower going up in Miami. In Providence, Rhode Island, his firm built a shopping mall that required one of the largest steel mill orders placed on the East Coast (more than twenty-four thousand tons); it is also involved in perhaps the biggest commercial project in the world—the Meadowlands Xanadu entertainment and sports complex in East Rutherford, New Jersey, which will house a stadium for the New York Giants and New York Jets football teams, a three-thousand-seat music theater, the country's largest movie multiplex, and the SnowPark, the nation's first indoor ski resort. For most of the past several years, McNamara/Salvia's engineers have worked on fifty to sixty projects annually, an average of one new building a week. And they have never had a building come even close to collapsing.

So I asked Salvia at his office in downtown Boston how he has ensured that the buildings he works on are designed and con-

structed right. Joe Salvia is sixty-one, with almost no hair, a strong
Boston accent, and a cheery, take-your-time, how-about-some-
coffee manner that I didn't expect from an engineer. He told me
about the first project he ever designed—a roof for a small shopping plaza.

He was just out of college, a twenty-three-year-old kid from
East Cambridge, which is not exactly where the Harvard professors live. His father was a maintenance man and his mother
worked in a meat processing plant, but he was good in school
and became the first member of his family to go to college. He
went to Tufts University planning to become a doctor. Then he
hit organic chemistry class.

"They said, 'Here, we want you to memorize these form-
ulas,'" he explained. "I said, 'Why do I have to memorize them if
I know where the book is?' They said, 'You want to be a doctor?
That's what you have to do in medicine—you have to memorize
everything.' That seemed ridiculous to me. Plus I wasn't good at
memorizing. So I quit."

But Salvia was good at solving complex problems—he tried
to explain how he solves quadratic equations in his head, though
all I managed to pick up was that I'd never before heard someone
say "quadratic equation" in a Boston accent. "I also liked the concept of creating," he said. As a result, he switched to engineering,
a scientific but practical field, and he loved it. He learned, as he
put it, "basic statics and dynamics—you know, F equals ma," and
he learned about the chemistry and physics of steel, concretes,
and soil.

But he'd built nothing when he graduated with his bachelor's
degree and joined Sumner Shane, an architectural engineering
firm that specialized in structural engineering for shopping

centers. One of its projects was a new shopping mall in Texas, and Salvia was assigned the roof system. He found he actually understood a lot about how to build a solid roof from his textbooks and from the requirements detailed in building codes.

"I knew from college how to design with structural steel— how to use beams and columns," he said. And the local building codes spelled out what was required for steel strength, soil composition, snow-bearing capacity, wind-pressure resistance, and earthquake tolerance. All he had to do was factor these elements into the business deal, which specified the size of the building, the number of floors, the store locations, the loading docks. As we talked he was already drawing the contours for me on a piece of paper. It started out as a simple rectangle. Then he sketched in the store walls, doorways, walking space. The design began taking form.

"You draw a grid of likely locations to carry the roof weight," he said, and he put in little crosses where columns could be placed. "The rest is algebra," he said. "You solve for X." You calculate the weight of the roof from its size and thickness, and then, given columns placed every thirty feet, say, you calculate the diameter and strength of the column required. You check your math to make sure you've met all the requirements.

All this he had learned in college. But, he discovered, there was more—much more—that they hadn't taught him in school.

"You know the geometric theory of what is best, but not the practical theory of what can be done," he said. There was the matter of cost, for example, about which he had not a clue. The size and type of materials he put in changed the cost of the project, it turned out. There was also the matter of aesthetics, the desires of a client who didn't want a column standing in the middle of a floor, for instance, or blocking a particular sightline.

"If engineers were in charge, every building would be a rectangular box," Salvia said. Instead, every building is new and individual in ways both small and large—they are complex—and as a result there is often no textbook formula for the problems that come up. Later, for example, when he established his own firm, he and his team did the structural engineering for Boston's International Place, a landmark forty-six-story steel and glass tower designed by the architect Philip Johnson. The building was unusual, a cylinder smashed against a rectangle, a form that hadn't been tried in a skyscraper before. From a structural engineering point of view, Salvia explained, cylinders are problematic. A square provides 60 percent more stiffness than a circle, and in wind or an earthquake a building needs to be able to resist the tendency to twist or bend. But a distorted cylinder it was, and he and his team had to invent the engineering to realize Johnson's aesthetic vision.

Salvia's first mall roof may have been a simpler proposition, but it seemed to him at the time to have no end of difficulties. Besides the concerns of costs and aesthetics, he also needed to deal with the requirements of all the other professionals involved. There were the plumbing engineers, the electrical engineers, the mechanical engineers—every one of them wanting to put pipes, wiring, HVAC units just where his support columns were supposed to go.

"A building is like a body," he said. It has a skin. It has a skeleton. It has a vascular system—the plumbing. It has a breathing system—the ventilation. It has a nervous system—the wiring. All together, he explained, projects today involve some sixteen different trades. He pulled out the construction plans for a four-hundred-foot-tall skyscraper he was currently building and flipped to the table of contents to show me. Each trade had contributed its own separate section. There were sections for conveying systems (elevators and escalators), mechanical systems (heating, ventilation, plumbing, air conditioning, fire protection), masonry, concrete structures, metal structures, electrical systems, doors and windows, thermal and moisture systems (including waterproofing and insulation), rough and finish carpentry, site work (including excavation, waste and storm water collection, and walkways)—everything right down to the carpeting, painting, landscaping, and rodent control.

All the separate contributions had to be included. Yet they also had to fit together somehow so as to make sense as a whole. And then they had to be executed precisely and in coordination. On the face of it, the complexities seemed overwhelming. To manage them, Salvia said, the entire industry was forced to evolve.

For most of modern history, he explained, going back to medieval times, the dominant way people put up buildings was by going out and hiring Master Builders who designed them, engineered them, and oversaw construction from start to finish, portico to plumbing. Master Builders built Notre Dame, St. Peter's Basilica, and the United States Capitol building. But by the middle of the twentieth century the Master Builders were dead and gone. The variety and sophistication of advancements in every stage of the construction process had overwhelmed the abilities of any individual to master them.

In the first division of labor, architectural and engineering design split off from construction. Then, piece by piece, each component became further specialized and split off, until there were architects on one side, often with their own areas of sub-specialty, and engineers on another, with their various kinds of expertise; the builders, too, fragmented into their own multiple divisions, ranging from tower crane contractors to finish carpenters. The field looked, in other words, a lot like medicine, with all its specialists and superspecialists.

Yet we in medicine continue to exist in a system created in the Master Builder era—a system in which a lone Master Physician with a prescription pad, an operating room, and a few people to follow his lead plans and executes the entirety of care for a patient, from diagnosis through treatment. We've been slow to adapt to the reality that, for example, a third of patients have at least ten specialist physicians actively involved in their care by their last year of life, and probably a score more personnel, ranging from nurse practitioners and physician assistants to pharmacists and home medical aides. And the evidence of how slow we've been to adapt is the extraordinarily high rate at which care for patients is duplicated or flawed or completely uncoordinated.

In the construction business, Salvia explained, such failure is not an option. No matter how complex the problems he faced in designing that first shopping mall roof, he very quickly understood that he had no margin for error. Perhaps it's the large number of people who would die if his roof collapsed under the weight of snow. Or perhaps it's the huge amount of money that would be lost in the inevitable lawsuits. But, whatever the reason, architects, engineers, and builders were forced long ago—going back to the early part of the last century—to confront the fact that the Master Builder model no longer worked. So they abandoned it. They found a different way to make sure they get things right.

To show me what they do, Salvia had me come to see one of the construction sites where he and his team were working. His firm happened to have a job under way a short, sunny walk from his office. The Russia Wharf building was going to be a sprawling thirty-two-story, 700,000-square-foot office and apartment complex. Its footprint alone was two acres.

The artistic renderings were spectacular. Russia Wharf was where merchant ships sailing between St. Petersburg and Boston with iron, hemp, and canvas for the shipbuilding industry once docked. The Boston Tea Party took place next door. The new glass and steel building was going up right along this waterfront, with a ten-story atrium underneath and the 110-year-old brick facades of the original Classical Revival structures preserved as part of the new building.

When I arrived for the tour, Salvia took one look at my blue Brooks Brothers blazer and black penny loafers and let out a low chuckle.

"One thing you learn going to construction sites is you have to have the right shoes," he said.

The insides of the old buildings had long been gutted and the steel skeleton of the new tower had been built almost halfway up, to the fourteenth floor. A tower crane hung four stories above the structure. Ants on the ground, we worked our way around a pair of concrete mixing trucks, the cops stopping traffic, and a few puddles of gray mud to enter the first-floor field office of John Moriarty and Associates, the general contractor for the project. It was nothing like the movie construction-site field trailers I had in my mind—no rusting coffee urn, no cheap staticky radio playing, no cigar-chewing boss barking orders. Instead, there were half a dozen offices where men and women, many in work boots, jeans, and yellow safety reflector vests, sat staring into computer terminals or were gathered around a conference table with a PowerPoint slide up on a screen.

I was given a blue hard hat and an insurance release to sign and introduced to Finn O'Sullivan, a smiling six-foot-three Irishman with a lilting brogue who served as the "project executive" for the building—they don't call them field bosses anymore, I was told. O'Sullivan said that on any given day he has between two and five hundred workers on-site, including people from any of sixty sub-contractors. The volume of knowledge and degree of complexity he had to manage, it struck me, were as monstrous as anything I had encountered in medicine. He tried to explain how he and his colleagues made sure that all those people were doing their work correctly, that the building would come together properly, despite the enormous number of considerations—and despite the fact that he could not possibly understand the particulars of most of the tasks involved. But I didn't really get his explanation until he brought me to the main conference room. There, on the walls around a big white oval table, hung sheets of butcher-block-size printouts of what were, to my surprise, checklists.

Along the right wall as we walked in was, O'Sullivan explained, the construction schedule. As I peered in close, I saw a line-by-line, day-by-day listing of every building task that needed to be accomplished, in what order, and when—the fifteenth-floor concrete pour on the thirteenth of the month, a steel delivery on the fourteenth, and so on. The schedule spread over multiple sheets. There was special color coding, with red items highlighting critical steps that had to be done before other steps could proceed. As each task was accomplished, a job supervisor reported to O'Sullivan, who then put a check mark in his computer scheduling program. He posted a new printout showing the next phase of work each week, sometimes more frequently if things were moving along. The construction schedule was essentially one long checklist.

Since every building is a new creature with its own particularities, every building checklist is new, too. It is drawn up by a group of people representing each of the sixteen trades, including, in this case, someone from Salvia's firm making sure the structural engineering steps were incorporated as they should be. Then the whole checklist is sent to the subcontractors and other independent experts so they can double-check that everything is correct, that nothing has been missed.

What results is remarkable: a succession of day-by-day checks that guide how the building is constructed and ensure that the knowledge of hundreds, perhaps thousands, is put to use in the right place at the right time in the right way.

The construction schedule for the Russia Wharf project was designed to build the complex up in layers, and I could actually see those layers when Bernie Rouillard, Salvia's lead structural engineer for the project, took me on a tour. I should mention here that I am not too fond of heights. But I put on my hard hat and followed Rouillard—past the signs that said WARNING: CONSTRUCTION PERSONNEL ONLY, around a rusting nest of discarded rebar, over a trail of wood planks that served as a walkway into the building, and then into an orange cage elevator that rattled its way up the side of the skeleton to the fourteenth floor. We stepped out onto a vast, bare, gray slab floor with no walls, just twelve-foot vertical steel columns ringing the outside, a massive rectangular concrete core in the center, and the teeming city surrounding us.

"You can see everything from here," Rouillard said, beckoning me to join him out on the edge. I crept to within three feet and tried not to dwell on the wind whipping through us or the vertiginous distance to the ground as he good-naturedly pointed out the sites along the waterfront below. I did better when we turned our backs to the city and he showed me the bare metal trusses that had been put into the ceiling to support the floor being built above.

Next, he said, will come the fireproofers.

"You have to fireproof metal?" I asked.

Oh yes, he said. In a fire, the metal can plasticize—lose its stiffness and bend like spaghetti. This was why the World Trade Center buildings collapsed, he said. He walked me down a stairway to the floor below us. Here, I could see, the fireproofing material had been sprayed on, a gypsum-based substance that made the ceiling trusses look gray and woolly.

We went down a couple more floors and he showed me that the "skin" of the building had now been hung at those levels. The tall, shiny glass and steel exterior had been bolted into the concrete floors every few feet. The farther down we went, the more the layers had advanced. One team of subcontractors had put up walls inside the skin. The pipefitters had then put in water and drainage pipes. The tin knockers followed and installed the ventilation ducts. By the time we got down to the lowest floors, the masonry, electrical wiring, plumbing, and even some fixtures like staircase railings were all in place. The whole intricate process was astounding to behold.

On the upper floors, however, I couldn't help but notice something that didn't look right, even to my untrained eyes. There had been rain recently and on each of the open floors large amounts of water had pooled in the same place—up against the walls of the inner concrete core. It was as if the floor were tilted inward, like a bowl. I asked Rouillard about this.

"Yeah, the owners saw that and they weren't too happy," he said. He explained what he thinks had happened. The immense weight of the concrete core combined with the particular makeup of the soil underneath had probably caused the core to settle sooner than anticipated. Meanwhile, the outer steel frame had not yet been loaded with weight—there were still eighteen stories to be built upon it—and that's why he believes the floor had begun to tip inward. Once the steel frame was loaded, he fully expected the floor to level out.

The fascinating thing to me wasn't his explanation. I had no idea what to make of his answer. But here was a situation that hadn't been anticipated on the construction checklist: the tilting of the upper floors. At a minimum, a water cleanup would be needed and the schedule adjusted for it. That alone could throw the builders' tidy plans off track. Furthermore, the people involved had to somehow determine whether the tilting indicated a serious construction defect. I was curious to know how they handled this question, for there was inevitable uncertainty. How could they know that the problem was just ordinary settling, that loading the steel frame would in fact level out the floor? As Rouillard acknowledged, "variances can occur." This was a situation of true complexity.

Back down in the field office, I asked Finn O'Sullivan how he and his team dealt with such a circumstance. After all, skyscraper builders must run into thousands like it—difficulties they could never have predicted or addressed in a checklist designed in advance. The medical way of dealing with such problems—with the inevitable nuances of an individual patient case—is to leave them to the expert's individual judgment. You give the specialist autonomy. In this instance, Rouillard was the specialist. Had the building site been a hospital ward, his personal judgment would hold sway.

This approach has a flaw, however, O'Sullivan pointed out. Like a patient, a building involves multiple specialists—the sixteen trades. In the absence of a true Master Builder—a supreme, all-knowing expert with command of all existing knowledge—autonomy is a disaster. It produces only a cacophony of incompatible decisions and overlooked errors. You get a building that doesn't stand up straight. This sounded to me like medicine at its worst.

So what do you do? I asked.

That was when O'Sullivan showed me a different piece of paper hanging in his conference room. Pinned to the left-hand wall opposite the construction schedule was another butcher-block-size sheet almost identical in form, except this one, O'Sullivan said, was called a "submittal schedule." It was also a checklist, but it didn't specify construction tasks; it specified *communication* tasks. For the way the project managers dealt with the unexpected and the uncertain was by making sure the experts spoke to one another—on X date regarding Y process. The experts could make their individual judgments, but they had to do so as part of a team that took one another's concerns into account, discussed unplanned developments, and agreed on the way forward. While no one could anticipate all the problems, they could foresee where and when they might occur. The checklist therefore detailed who had to talk to whom, by which date, and about what aspect of construction—who had to share (or "submit") particular kinds of information before the next steps could proceed.

The submittal schedule specified, for instance, that by the end of the month the contractors, installers, and elevator engineers had to review the condition of the elevator cars traveling up to the tenth floor. The elevator cars were factory constructed and tested. They were installed by experts. But it was not assumed that they would work perfectly. Quite the opposite. The assumption was that anything could go wrong, anything could get missed. What? Who knows? That's the nature of complexity. But it was also assumed that, if you got the right people together and had them take a moment to talk things over as a team rather than as individuals, serious problems could be identified and averted.

So the submittal schedule made them talk. The contractors had to talk with the installers and elevator engineers by the thirty-first. They had to talk about fire protection with the fireproofers by the twenty-fifth. And two weeks earlier, they had been required to talk about the condition of the core wall and flooring on the upper floors, where the water had pooled, with the structural engineers, a consultant, and the owners.

I saw that the box had been checked. The task was done. I asked Rouillard how the discussion had gone.

Very well, he said. Everyone met and reviewed the possibilities. The owners and the contractors were persuaded that it was reasonable to expect the floor to level out. Cleanup was arranged, the schedule was adjusted, and everyone signed off.

In the face of the unknown—the always nagging uncertainty about whether, under complex circumstances, things will really be okay—the builders trusted in the power of communication. They didn't believe in the wisdom of the single individual, of even an experienced engineer. They believed in the wisdom of the group, the wisdom of making sure that multiple pairs of eyes were on a problem and then letting the watchers decide what to do.

Man is fallible, but maybe men are less so.

In a back room of the field office, Ryan Walsh, a buzz-cut young man of about thirty wearing a yellow reflector vest, sat in front of two big flat-screen displays. His job, he explained, was to take all the construction plans submitted by each of the major trades and merge them into a three-dimensional floor-by-floor computer rendering of the building. He showed me what the top floor looked like on the screen. He'd so far loaded in the specifications from nine of the trades—the structural specs, the elevator specs, the plumbing specs, and so on. He used his mouse to walk us through the building as if we were taking a stroll down the corridors. You could see the walls, the doors, the safety valves, everything. More to the point, you could see problems—a place where there wasn't enough overhead clearance for an average-size person, for example. He showed me an application called Clash Detective that ferreted out every instance in which the different specs conflicted with one another or with building regulations.

"If a structural beam is going where a lighting fixture is supposed to hang, the Clash Detective turns that beam a different color on-screen," he said. "You can turn up hundreds of clashes. I once found two thousand." But it's not enough to show the clash on the screen, he explained. You have to resolve it, and to do that you have to make sure the critical people talk. So the computer also flags the issue for the submittal schedule printout and sends an e-mail to each of the parties who have to resolve it.

There's yet another program, called ProjectCenter, that allows anyone who has found a problem—even a frontline worker—to e-mail all the relevant parties, track progress, and make sure a check is added to the schedule to confirm that everyone has talked and resolved the matter. When we were back at the McNamara/Salvia offices, Bernie Rouillard showed me one such e-mail he'd gotten that week. A worker had attached a digital photo of a twelve-foot steel I beam he was bolting in. It hadn't lined up properly and only two of the four bolts could fit. Was that all right, the worker wanted to know? No, Rouillard wrote back. They worked out a solution together: to weld the beam into place. The e-mail was also automatically sent to the main contractor and anyone else who might potentially be required to sign off. Each party was given three days to confirm that the proposed solution was okay. And everyone needed to confirm they'd communicated, since the time taken for even this small fix could change the entire sequence in which other things needed to be done.

Joe Salvia had earlier told me that the major advance in the science of construction over the last few decades has been the perfection of tracking and communication. But only now did I understand what he meant.

The building world's willingness to apply its strategies to difficulties of any size and seriousness is striking. Salvia's partner, Robert

McNamara, for instance, was one of the structural engineers for the Citicorp (now Citigroup) building in midtown Manhattan, with its iconic slanted rooftop. It was planned to rise more than nine hundred feet on four nine-story-tall stiltlike columns placed not at the building's corners but at the center of each side and steadied by giant, hidden chevron-shaped braces designed by William LeMessurier, the project's lead structural engineer. The visual effect was arresting. The colossal structure would look like it was almost floating above Fifty-third Street. But wind-tunnel testing of a model revealed that the skyscraper stood so high above the surrounding buildings in midtown that it was subject to wind streams and turbulence with forces familiar only to airplane designers, not to structural engineers. The acceptable amount of sway for the building was unknown.

So what did they do? They did not scrap the building or shrink it to a less ambitious size. Instead, McNamara proposed a novel solution called a "tuned mass damper." They could, he suggested, suspend an immense four-hundred-ton concrete block from huge springs in the building's crown on the fifty-ninth floor, so that when wind pitched the building one way, the block would swing the other way and steady it.

The solution was brilliant and elegant. The engineers did some wind-tunnel testing with a small model of the design, and the results were highly reassuring. Nonetheless, some chance of error and unpredictability always remains in projects of this complexity. So the builders reduced their margin of error the best way they knew how—by taking a final moment to make sure that everyone talked it through as a group. The building owner met with the architect, someone from the city buildings department, the structural engineers, and others. They reviewed the idea and all the calculations behind it. They confirmed that every concern they could think of had been addressed. Then they signed off on the plan, and the skyscraper was built.

It is unnerving to think that we allow buildings this difficult to design and construct to go up in the midst of our major cities, with thousands of people inside and tens of thousands more living and working nearby. Doing so seems risky and unwise. But we allow it based on trust in the ability of the experts to manage the complexities. They in turn know better than to rely on their individual abilities to get everything right. They trust instead in one set of checklists to make sure that simple steps are not missed or skipped and in another set to make sure that everyone talks through and resolves all the hard and unexpected problems.

"The biggest cause of serious error in this business is a failure of communication," O'Sullivan told me.

In the Citicorp building, for example, the calculations behind the designs for stabilizing the building assumed the joints in those giant braces at the base of the building would be welded. Joint welding, however, is labor intensive and therefore expensive. Bethlehem Steel, which took the contract to erect the tower, proposed switching to bolted joints, which are not as strong. They calculated that the bolts would do the job. But, as a *New Yorker* story later uncovered, their calculations were somehow not reviewed with LeMessurier. That checkpoint was bypassed.

It is not certain that a review would have led him to recognize a problem at the time. But in 1978, a year after the building opened, LeMessurier, prompted by a question from a Princeton engineering student, discovered the change. And he found it had produced a fatal flaw: the building would not be able to withstand seventy-mile-an-hour winds—which, according to weather tables, would occur at least once every fifty-five years in New York City. In that circumstance, the joints would fail and the building would collapse, starting on the thirtieth floor. By now, the tower was fully occupied. LeMessurier broke the news to the owners and to city officials. And that summer, as Hurricane Ella made its way toward the city, an emergency crew worked at night under veil of secrecy to weld two-inch-thick steel plates around the two hundred critical bolts, and the building was secured. The Citicorp tower has stood solidly ever since.

The construction industry's checklist process has clearly not been foolproof at catching problems. Nonetheless, its record of success has been astonishing. In the United States, we have nearly five million commercial buildings, almost one hundred million low-rise homes, and eight million or so high-rise residences. We add somewhere around seventy thousand new commercial buildings and one million new homes each year. But "building failure"—defined as a partial or full collapse of a functioning structure—is exceedingly rare, especially for skyscrapers. According to a 2003 Ohio State University study, the United States experiences an average of just twenty serious "building failures" per year. That's an annual avoidable failure rate of less than 0.00002 percent. And, as Joe Salvia explained to me, although buildings are now more complex and sophisticated than ever in history, with higher standards expected for everything from earthquake proofing to energy efficiency, they take a third less time to build than they did when he started his career.

The checklists work.

4. THE IDEA

There is a particularly tantalizing aspect to the building industry's strategy for getting things right in complex situations: it's that it gives people power. In response to risk, most authorities tend to centralize power and decision making. That's usually what checklists are about—dictating instructions to the workers below to ensure they do things the way we want. Indeed, the first building checklist I saw, the construction schedule on the right-hand wall of O'Sullivan's conference room, was exactly that. It spelled out to the tiniest detail every critical step the tradesmen were expected to follow and when—which is logical if you're confronted with simple and routine problems; you want the forcing function.

But the list on O'Sullivan's other wall revealed an entirely different philosophy about power and what should happen to it when you're confronted with complex, nonroutine problems—such as what to do when a difficult, potentially dangerous, and unanticipated anomaly suddenly appears on the fourteenth floor of a thirty-two-story skyscraper under construction. The philosophy is that you push the power of decision making out to the periphery and away from the center. You give people the room to adapt, based on their experience and expertise. All you ask is that they talk to one another and take responsibility. That is what works.

The strategy is unexpectedly democratic, and it has become standard nowadays, O'Sullivan told me, even in building inspections. The inspectors do not recompute the wind-force calculations or decide whether the joints in a given building should be bolted or welded, he said. Determining whether a structure like Russia Wharf or my hospital's new wing is built to code and fit for occupancy involves more knowledge and complexity than any one inspector could possibly have. So although inspectors do what they can to oversee a building's construction, mostly they make certain the builders have the proper checks in place and then have them sign affidavits attesting that they themselves have ensured that the structure is up to code. Inspectors disperse the power and the responsibility.

"It makes sense," O'Sullivan said. "The inspectors have more troubles with the safety of a two-room addition from a do-it-yourselfer than they do with projects like ours. So that's where they focus their efforts." Also, I suspect, at least some authorities have recognized that when they don't let go of authority they fail. We need look no further than what happened after Hurricane Katrina hit New Orleans.

At 6:00 a.m., on August 29, 2005, Katrina made landfall in

Plaquemines Parish in New Orleans. The initial reports were falsely reassuring. With telephone lines, cell towers, and electrical power down, the usual sources of information were unavailable. By afternoon, the levees protecting the city had been breached. Much of New Orleans was under water. The evidence was on television, but Michael Brown, the director of the Federal Emergency Management Agency, discounted it and told a press conference that the situation was largely under control.

FEMA was relying on information from multiple sources, but only one lone agent was actually present in New Orleans. That agent had managed to get a Coast Guard helicopter ride over the city that first afternoon, and he filed an urgent report the only way he could with most communication lines cut—by e-mail. Flooding was widespread, the e-mail said; he himself had seen bodies floating in the water and hundreds of people stranded on rooftops. Help was needed. But the government's top officials did not use e-mail. And as a Senate hearing uncovered, they were not apprised of the contents of the message until the next day.

By then, 80 percent of the city was flooded. Twenty thousand refugees were stranded at the New Orleans Superdome. Another twenty thousand were at the Ernest N. Morial Convention Center. Over five thousand people were at an overpass on Interstate 10, some of them left by rescue crews and most carrying little more than the clothes on their backs. Hospitals were without power and suffering horrendous conditions. As people became desperate for food and water, looting began. Civil breakdown became a serious concern.

Numerous local officials and impromptu organizers made efforts to contact authorities and let them know what was needed, but they too were unable to reach anyone. When they finally got a live person on the phone, they were told to wait—their requests would have to be sent up the line. The traditional command-and-control system rapidly became overwhelmed. There were too many decisions to be made and too little information about precisely where and what help was needed.

Nevertheless, the authorities refused to abandon the traditional model. For days, while conditions deteriorated hourly, arguments roared over who had the power to provide the resources and make decisions. The federal government wouldn't yield the power to the state government. The state government wouldn't give it to the local government. And no one would give it to people in the private sector.

The result was a combination of anarchy and Orwellian bureaucracy with horrifying consequences. Trucks with water and food were halted or diverted or refused entry by authorities—the supplies were not part of their plan. Bus requisitions were held up for days; the official request did not even reach the U.S. Department of Transportation until two days after tens of thousands had become trapped and in need of evacuation. Meanwhile two hundred local transit buses were sitting idle on higher ground nearby.

The trouble wasn't a lack of sympathy among top officials. It was a lack of understanding that, in the face of an extraordinarily complex problem, power needed to be pushed out of the center as far as possible. Everyone was waiting for the cavalry, but a centrally run, government-controlled solution was not going to be possible.

Asked afterward to explain the disastrous failures, Michael Chertoff, secretary of Homeland Security, said that it had been an "ultra-catastrophe," a "perfect storm" that "exceeded the foresight of the planners, and maybe anybody's foresight." But that's not an explanation. It's simply the definition of a complex situation. And such a situation requires a different kind of solution from the command-and-control paradigm officials relied on.

Of all organizations, it was oddly enough Wal-Mart that best recognized the complex nature of the circumstances, according to a case study from Harvard's Kennedy School of Government. Briefed on what was developing, the giant discount retailer's chief executive officer, Lee Scott, issued a simple edict. "This company will respond to the level of this disaster," he was remembered to have said in a meeting with his upper management. "A lot of you are going to have to make decisions above your level. Make the best decision that you can with the information that's available to you at the time, and, above all, do the right thing."

As one of the officers at the meeting later recalled, "That was it." The edict was passed down to store managers and set the tone for how people were expected to react. On the most immediate level, Wal-Mart had 126 stores closed due to damage and power outages. Twenty thousand employees and their family members were displaced. The initial focus was on helping them. And within forty-eight hours, more than half of the damaged stores were up and running again. But according to one executive on the scene, as word of the disaster's impact on the city's population began filtering in from Wal-Mart employees on the ground, the priority shifted from reopening stores to "Oh, my God, what can we do to help these people?"

Acting on their own authority, Wal-Mart's store managers began distributing diapers, water, baby formula, and ice to residents. Where FEMA still hadn't figured out how to requisition supplies, the managers fashioned crude paper-slip credit systems for first responders, providing them with food, sleeping bags, toiletries, and also, where available, rescue equipment like hatchets, ropes, and boots. The assistant manager of a Wal-Mart store engulfed by a thirty-foot storm surge ran a bulldozer through the store, loaded it with any items she could salvage, and gave them all away in the parking lot. When a local hospital told her it was running short of drugs, she went back in and broke into the store's pharmacy—and was lauded by upper management for it.

Senior Wal-Mart officials concentrated on setting goals, measuring progress, and maintaining communication lines with employees at the front lines and with official agencies when they could. In other words, to handle this complex situation, they did not issue instructions. Conditions were too unpredictable and constantly changing. They worked on making sure people talked. Wal-Mart's emergency operations team even included a member of the Red Cross. (The federal government declined Wal-Mart's invitation to participate.) The team also opened a twenty-four-hour call center for employees, which started with eight operators but rapidly expanded to eighty to cope with the load.

Along the way, the team discovered that, given common goals to do what they could to help and to coordinate with one another, Wal-Mart's employees were able to fashion some extraordinary solutions. They set up three temporary mobile pharmacies in the city and adopted a plan to provide medications for free at all of their stores for evacuees with emergency needs—even without a prescription. They set up free check cashing for payroll and other checks in disaster-area stores. They opened temporary clinics to provide emergency personnel with inoculations against flood-borne illnesses. And most prominently, within just two days of Katrina's landfall, the company's logistics teams managed to contrive ways to get tractor trailers with food, water, and emergency equipment past roadblocks and into the dying city. They were able to supply water and food to refugees and even to the National Guard a day before the government appeared on the scene. By the end Wal-Mart had sent in a total of 2,498 trailer loads of emergency supplies and donated $3.5 million in merchandise to area shelters and command centers.

"If the American government had responded like Wal-Mart has responded, we wouldn't be in this crisis," Jefferson Parish's top official, Aaron Broussard, said in a network television interview at the time.

The lesson of this tale has been misunderstood. Some have argued that the episode proves that the private sector is better than the public sector in handling complex situations. But it isn't. For every Wal-Mart, you can find numerous examples of major New Orleans businesses that proved inadequately equipped to respond to the unfolding events—from the utility corporations, which struggled to get the telephone and electrical lines working, to the oil companies, which kept too little crude oil and refinery capacity on hand for major disruptions. Public officials could also claim some genuine successes. In the early days of the crisis, for example, the local police and firefighters, lacking adequate equipment, recruited an armada of Louisiana sportsmen with flat-bottom boats and orchestrated a breathtaking rescue of more than sixty-two thousand people from the water, rooftops, and attics of the deluged city.

No, the real lesson is that under conditions of true complexity—where the knowledge required exceeds that of any individual and unpredictability reigns—efforts to dictate every step from the center will fail. People need room to act and adapt. Yet they cannot succeed as isolated individuals, either—that is anarchy. Instead, they require a seemingly contradictory mix of freedom and expectation—expectation to coordinate, for example, and also to measure progress toward common goals.

This was the understanding people in the skyscraper-building industry had grasped. More remarkably, they had learned to codify that understanding into simple checklists. They had made the reliable management of complexity a routine.

That routine requires balancing a number of virtues: freedom and discipline, craft and protocol, specialized ability and group collaboration. And for checklists to help achieve that balance, they have to take two almost opposing forms. They supply a set of checks to ensure the stupid but critical stuff is not overlooked, and they supply another set of checks to ensure people talk and coordinate and accept responsibility while nonetheless being left the power to manage the nuances and unpredictabilities the best they know how.

I came away from Katrina and the builders with a kind of theory: under conditions of complexity, not only are checklists a help, they are *required* for success. There must always be room for judgment, but judgment aided—and even enhanced—by procedure.

Having hit on this "theory," I began to recognize checklists in odd corners everywhere—in the hands of professional football coordinators, say, or on stage sets. Listening to the radio, I heard the story behind rocker David Lee Roth's notorious insistence that Van Halen's contracts with concert promoters contain a clause specifying that a bowl of M&M's has to be provided backstage, but with every single brown candy removed, upon pain of forfeiture of the show, with full compensation to the band. And at least once, Van Halen followed through, peremptorily canceling a show in Colorado when Roth found some brown M&M's in his dressing room. This turned out to be, however, not another example of the insane demands of power-mad celebrities but an ingenious ruse.

As Roth explained in his memoir, *Crazy from the Heat*, "Van Halen was the first band to take huge productions into tertiary, third-level markets. We'd pull up with nine eighteen-wheeler trucks, full of gear, where the standard was three trucks, max. And there were many, many technical errors—whether it was the girders couldn't support the weight, or the flooring would sink in, or the doors weren't big enough to move the gear through. The contract rider read like a version of the Chinese Yellow Pages because there was so much equipment, and so many human beings to make it function." So just as a little test, buried somewhere in the middle of the rider, would be article 126, the no-brown-M&M's clause. "When I would walk backstage, if I saw a brown M&M in that bowl," he wrote, "well, we'd line-check the entire production. Guaranteed you're going to arrive at a technical error. . . . Guaranteed you'd run into a problem." These weren't trifles, the radio story pointed out. The mistakes could be life-threatening. In Colorado, the band found the local promoters had failed to read the weight requirements and the staging would have fallen through the arena floor.

"David Lee Roth had a checklist!" I yelled at the radio.

I ran my theory—about the necessity of checklists—by Jody

Adams, the chef and owner of Rialto, one of my favorite restaurants in Boston. In the early 1990s, *Food and Wine* magazine named her one of America's ten best new chefs, and in 1997 she won a James Beard Foundation Best Chef award, which is the Oscar for food. Rialto is frequently mentioned on national best-restaurant lists, most recently *Esquire* magazine's. Her focus is on regional Italian cuisine, though with a distinctive take.

Adams is self-taught. An anthropology major at Brown University, she never went to culinary school. "But I had a thing for food," as she puts it, and she went to work in restaurants, learning her way from chopping onions to creating her own style of cooking.

The level of skill and craft she has achieved in her restaurant is daunting. Moreover, she has sustained it for many years now. I was interested in how she did it. I understood perfectly well how the Burger Kings and Taco Bells of the world operate. They are driven by tightly prescribed protocol. They provide Taylorized, assembly-line food. But in great restaurants the food is ever-evolving, refined, and individual. Nevertheless, they have to produce an extraordinary level of excellence day after day, year after year, for one to three hundred people per night. I had my theory of how such perfectionism is accomplished, but was it true? Adams invited me in to see.

I spent one Friday evening perched on a stool in Rialto's long and narrow kitchen amid the bustle, the shouting, the grill flaming on one side, the deep fryer sizzling on another. Adams and her staff served 150 people in five hours. That night, they made a roasted tomato soup with sweated onions and garlic; squid ink ravioli filled with a salt cod brandade on a bed of squash blossoms and lobster sauce; grilled bluefish with corn relish, heirloom tomatoes, and pickled peppers; slow-roasted duck marinated in soy sauce, balsamic vinegar, mustard, rosemary, and garlic; and three dozen other mouthwatering dishes.

Sitting there, I saw remarkable expertise. Half of Adams's staff had been to culinary school. Few had less than a decade of experience. They each had a kitchen specialty. There was a pastry chef, baker, grill chef, fry cook, dessert chef, sous chef, sommelier—you get the picture. Through the years, they had perfected their technique. I couldn't fathom the subtleties of most of what they did. Though I am a surgeon, they wouldn't let me anywhere near their knives. Jay, the pasta chef, showed me how to heat butter properly and tell by sight when gnocchi were perfectly boiled. Adams showed me how much a pinch of salt really was.

People celebrate the technique and creativity of cooking. Chefs are personalities today, and their daring culinary exploits are what make the television cooking shows so popular. But as I saw at Rialto, it's discipline—uncelebrated and untelevised—that keeps the kitchen clicking. And sure enough, checklists were at the center of that discipline.

First there was the recipe—the most basic checklist of all. Every dish had one. The recipes were typed out, put in clear plastic sleeves, and placed at each station. Adams was religious about her staff's using them. Even for her, she said, "following the recipe is essential to making food of consistent quality over time."

Tacked to a bulletin board beside the dessert station was what Adams called her Kitchen Notes—e-mails to the staff of her brief observations about the food. The most recent was from 12:50 the previous night. "Fritters—more herbs, more garlic . . . more punch," it said. "Corn silk in corn! Creamed corn side on oval plates—not square! Mushrooms—more shallots, garlic, and marsala. USE THE RECIPES!"

The staff didn't always love following the recipes. You make the creamed corn a few hundred times and you believe you have it down. But that's when things begin to slip, Adams said.

The recipes themselves were not necessarily static. All the ones I saw had scribbled modifications in the margins—many of them improvements provided by staff. Sometimes there would be a wholesale revamp.

One new dish they were serving was a split whole lobster in a cognac and fish broth reduction with littleneck clams and chorizo. The dish is Adams's take on a famous Julia Child recipe. Before putting a dish on the menu, however, she always has the kitchen staff make a few test runs, and some problems emerged. Her recipe called for splitting a lobster and then sautéing it in olive oil. But the results proved too variable. Too often the lobster meat was either overcooked or undercooked. The sauce was also made to order, but it took too long for the eight-to-ten-minute turnaround that customers expect.

So she and two of her chefs reengineered the dish. They decided to make the sauce in advance and parboil the lobster ahead of time, as well. On repeated test runs, the lobster came out perfectly. The recipe was rewritten.

There was also a checklist for every customer. When an order was placed up front, it was printed out on a slip back in the kitchen. The ticket specified the dishes ordered, the table number, the seat number, any preferences required by the customer or noted in a database from previous visits—food allergies, for instance, or how the steak should be cooked, or whether this was a special occasion like a birthday or a visit from a VIP whom Adams needed to go out and say hello to. The sous chef, who serves as a kind of field officer for operations, read the tickets off as they came in.

"Fire mushrooms. Fire mozz. Lobo on hold. Steak very well done, no gluten, on hold."

"Fire" meant cook it now. "On hold" meant it was a second course. "Lobo" was the lobster. The steak needed to be cooked all the way through and the customer had a gluten allergy. A read-back was expected to confirm that the line cooks had heard the order right.

"Fire mushrooms. Fire mozz," said one.

"Lobo on hold," said the seafood cook.

"Steak very well done, no gluten, on hold," said the grill chef.

As in the construction world, however, not everything could be anticipated and reduced to a recipe. And so Adams, too, had developed a communication checklist to ensure people recognized, and dealt with, unexpected problems as a team. At five o'clock, half an hour before opening, the staff holds what she calls the "pow wow." Everyone gathers in the kitchen for a quick check to discuss unanticipated issues and concerns—the unpredictable. The night I was there, they reviewed the reservation count, two menu changes, how to fill in for a sick staff member, and a sweet sixteen party with twenty girls who were delayed and going to arrive in the midst of the dinner rush. Everyone was given a chance to speak, and they made plans for what to do.

Of course, this still couldn't guarantee everything would go right. There remained plenty of sources of uncertainty and imperfection: a soup might be plated too early and allowed to cool, a quail might have too little sauce, a striped bass might come off the grill too dry. So Adams had one final check in place. Every plate had to be reviewed by either her or the sous chef before it left the kitchen for the dining room. They made sure the food looked the way it should, checked it against the order ticket, gave it a sniff or, with a clean spoon, maybe even a taste.

I counted the dishes as they went by. At least 5 percent were sent back. "This calamari has to be fried more," the sous chef told the fry cook. "We want more of a golden brown."

Later, I got to try some of the results. I had the fried olives, the grilled clams, the summer succotash, and a local farm green salad. I also had the lobster. The food was incredible. I left at midnight with my stomach full and my brain racing. Even here, in one of our most particularized and craft-driven enterprises—in a way, Adams's cooking is more art than science—checklists were required. Everywhere I looked, the evidence seemed to point to the same conclusion. There seemed no field or profession where checklists might not help. And that might even include my own.

5. THE FIRST TRY

In late 2006, a woman with a British accent and a Geneva telephone number called me. She said that she was from the World Health Organization and she wanted to see whether I might help them organize a group of people to solve a small problem. Officials were picking up indications that the volume of surgery was increasing worldwide and that a significant portion of the care was so unsafe as to be a public danger. So they wanted to develop a global program to reduce avoidable deaths and harm from surgery.

I believe my response was, "Um, how do you do that?"

"We'll have a meeting," she said.

I asked how much money they'd be devoting to the problem.

"Oh, there's no real money," she said.

I said no. I couldn't do it. I was busy.

But she knew what she was about. She said something along the lines of, "Oh, sorry. I thought you were supposed to be some kind of expert on patient safety in surgery. My mistake."

I agreed to help organize the meeting.

One of the benefits of joining up to work with WHO was gaining access to the health system reports and data from the organization's 193 member countries. And compiling the available numbers in surgery, my research team and I found that the WHO officials' impression was correct: the global volume of surgery had exploded. By 2004, surgeons were performing some 230 million major operations annually—one for every twenty-five human beings on the planet—and the numbers have likely continued to increase since then. The volume of surgery had grown so swiftly that, without anyone's quite realizing, it has come to exceed global totals for childbirth—only with a death rate ten to one hundred times higher. Although most of the time a given procedure goes just fine, often it doesn't: estimates of complication rates for hospital surgery range from 3 to 17 percent. While incisions have gotten smaller and recoveries have gotten quicker, the risks remain serious. Worldwide, at least seven million people a year are left disabled and at least one million dead—a level of harm that approaches that of malaria, tuberculosis, and other traditional public health concerns.

Peering at the numbers, I understood why WHO—an organization devoted to solving large-scale public health problems—should suddenly have taken an interest in something as seemingly specific and high-tech as surgical care. Improvement in global economic conditions in recent decades had produced greater longevity and therefore a greater need for essential surgical services—for people with cancers, broken bones and other traumatic injuries, complications during child delivery, major birth defects, disabling kidney stones and gallstones and hernias. Although there remained some two billion people, especially in rural areas, without access to a surgeon, health systems in all countries were now massively increasing the number of surgical procedures performed. As a result, the safety and quality of that care had become a major issue everywhere.

But what could be done about it? Remedying surgery as a public health matter is not like remedying, say, polio. I'd traveled with WHO physicians overseeing the campaign to eradicate polio globally and seen how hard just providing vaccines to a population could be. Surgery was drastically more complex. Finding ways to reduce its harm in a single hospital seemed difficult enough. Finding a way that could reach every operating room in the world seemed absurd. With more than twenty-five hundred different surgical procedures, ranging from brain biopsies to toe amputations, pacemaker insertions to spleen extractions, appendectomies to kidney transplants, you don't even know where to start. Perhaps, I thought, I could work with WHO to focus on reducing the harm of just one procedure—much like with central lines—but how much of a dent would that make in a problem of this scale?

In January 2007, at WHO headquarters in Geneva, we convened a two-day meeting of surgeons, anesthesiologists, nurses, safety experts, even patients from around the world to puzzle through what could be done. We had clinicians from top facilities in Europe, Canada, and the United States. We had the chief surgeon for the International Committee of the Red Cross, who had sent teams to treat sick and wounded refugees everywhere from Mogadishu to Indonesia. We had a father from Zambia whose daughter inadvertently suffocated from lack of oxygen during treatment. As the group told stories of their findings and experiences with surgery around the world, I became only more skeptical. How could we possibly attempt to address so many different issues in so many different places?

A medical officer in his forties from western Ghana, where cocoa growing and gold mining had brought a measure of prosperity, told of the conditions in his district hospital. No surgeon was willing to stay, he said. Ghana was suffering from a brain drain, losing many of its highest skilled citizens to better opportunities abroad. He told us his entire hospital had just three medical officers—general physicians with no surgical training. Nevertheless, when a patient arrives critically ill and bleeding after two days in labor, or sick and feverish from appendicitis, or with a collapsed lung after a motorbike crash, the untutored doctors do what they have to do. They operate.

"You must understand," he said. "I manage everything. I am the pediatrician, obstetrician, surgeon, everything." He had textbooks and a manual of basic surgical techniques. He had an untrained assistant who had learned how to give basic anesthesia. His hospital's equipment was rudimentary. The standards were poor. Things sometimes went wrong. But he was convinced doing something was better than doing nothing at all.

A Russian bioengineer spoke. He'd spent much of his career overseeing the supply and service of medical equipment to hospitals in different parts of the world, and he described dangerous problems in both high- and low-income settings: inadequately maintained surgical devices that have set fire to patients or electrocuted them; new technologies used incorrectly because teams had not received proper training; critical, lifesaving equipment that was locked away in a cabinet or missing when people needed it.

The chief of surgery for the largest hospital in Mongolia described shortages of pain control medications, and others from Asia, Africa, and the Middle East recounted the same. A New Zealand researcher spoke of terrifying death rates in poor countries from unsafe anesthesia, noting that although some places in Africa had fewer than one in five thousand patients die from general anesthesia, others had rates more than ten times worse, with one study in Togo showing one in 150 died. An anesthesiologist from India chimed in, tracing problems with anesthesia to the low respect most surgeons accord anesthetists. In her country, she said, they shout anesthetists down and disregard the safety issues that her colleagues raise. Medical students see this and decide not to go into anesthesiology. As a result, the most risky part of surgery—anesthesia—is done by untrained people far more often than the surgery itself. A nurse from Ireland joined the clamor. Nurses work under even worse conditions, she said. They are often ignored as members of the team, condescended to, or fired for raising concerns. She'd seen it in her home country, and from her colleagues abroad she knew it to be the experience of nurses internationally.

On the one hand, everyone firmly agreed: surgery is enormously valuable to people's lives everywhere and should be made more broadly available. Even under the grimmest conditions, it is frequently lifesaving. And in much of the world, the serious complication rates seem acceptably low—in the 5 to 15 percent range for hospital operations.

On the other hand, the idea that such rates are "acceptable" was hard to swallow. Each percentage point, after all, represented millions left disabled or dead. Studies in the United States alone had found that at least half of surgical complications were preventable. But the causes and contributors were of every possible variety. We needed to do something. What, though, wasn't clear.

Some suggested more training programs. The idea withered almost upon utterance. If these failures were problems in every country—indeed, very likely, in every hospital—no training program could be deployed widely enough to make a difference. There was neither the money nor the capacity.

We discussed incentive approaches, such as the pay-for-performance schemes recently initiated on a trial basis in the United States. In these programs, clinicians receive financial rewards for being more consistent about giving, say, heart attack patients the proper care or incur penalties for not doing so. The strategy has shown results, but the gains have been modest—the country's largest pay-for-performance trial, for example, registered just 2 to 4 percent improvement. Furthermore, the measurements required for incentive payments are not easy to obtain. They rely on clinicians' self-reported results, which are not always accurate. The results are also strongly affected by how sick patients are to begin with. One might be tempted, for example, to pay surgeons with higher complication rates less, but some might simply have sicker patients. The incentive programs have thus far been expensive, incremental, and of limited benefit. Taking them global was unimaginable.

The most straightforward thing for the group to do would

have been to formulate and publish under the WHO name a set of official standards for safe surgical care. It is the approach expert panels commonly take. Such guidelines could cover everything from measures to prevent infection in surgery to expectations for training and cooperation in operating rooms. This would be our Geneva Convention on Safe Surgery, our Helsinki Accord to Stop Operating Room Mayhem.

But one had only to take a walk through the dim concrete basement hallways of the otherwise soaring WHO headquarters to start doubting that plan. Down in the basement, while taking a shortcut between buildings, I saw pallet after pallet of two-hundred-page guideline books from other groups that had been summoned to make their expert pronouncements. There were guidelines stacked waist-high on malaria prevention, HIV/AIDS treatment, and influenza management, all shrink-wrapped against the gathering dust. The standards had been carefully written and were, I am sure, wise and well considered. Some undoubtedly raised the bar of possibility for achievable global standards. But in most cases, they had at best trickled out into the world. At the bedsides of patients in Bangkok and Brazzaville, Boston and Brisbane, little had changed.

I asked a WHO official whether the organization had a guidebook on how to carry out successful global public health programs. She regarded me with a look that a parent might give a toddler searching the dog's mouth for the thing that makes the barking noise. It's a cute idea but idiotic.

I searched anyway. I asked people around WHO for examples of public health interventions we could learn from. They came up with instances like the smallpox vaccination campaign that eradicated the scourge from the world in 1979 and the work of Dr. John Snow famously tracing a deadly 1854 London cholera outbreak to water in a public well. When the disease struck a London neighborhood that summer, two hundred people died in the first three days. Three-quarters of the area's residents fled in panic. Nonetheless, by the next week, some five hundred more died. The dominant belief was that diseases like cholera were caused by "miasmas"—putrefied air. But Snow, skeptical of the bad-air theory, made a map of where the deceased had lived and found them clustered around a single water source, a well in Soho's Broad Street. He interviewed the bereaved families about their habits. He made a careful statistical analysis of possible factors. And he concluded that contaminated water had caused the outbreak. (It was later discovered that the well had been dug next to a leaking cesspit.) Snow persuaded the local council to remove the water well's pump handle. This disabled the well, ended the spread of the disease, and also established the essential methods of outbreak investigation that infectious disease specialists follow to this day.

All the examples, I noticed, had a few attributes in common: They involved simple interventions—a vaccine, the removal of a pump handle. The effects were carefully measured. And the interventions proved to have widely transmissible benefits—what business types would term a large ROI (return on investment) or what Archimedes would have called, merely, leverage.

Thinking of these essential requirements—simple, measurable, transmissible—I recalled one of my favorite public health studies. It was a joint public health program conducted by the U.S. Centers for Disease Control and HOPE, a charitable organization in Pakistan, to address the perilous rates of premature death among children in the slums of Karachi. The squatter settlements surrounding the megacity contained more than four million people living under some of the most crowded and squalid conditions in the world. Sewage ran in the streets. Chronic poverty and food shortages left 30 to 40 percent of the children malnourished. Virtually all drinking water sources were contaminated. One child in ten died before age five—usually from diarrhea or acute respiratory infections.

The roots of these problems were deep and multifactorial. Besides inadequate water and sewage systems, illiteracy played a part, hampering the spread of basic health knowledge. Corruption, political instability, and bureaucracy discouraged investment in local industry that might provide jobs and money for families to improve their conditions. Low global agriculture prices made rural farming life impossible, causing hundreds of thousands to flock to the cities in search of work, which only increased the crowding. Under these circumstances, it seemed unlikely that any meaningful improvement in the health of children could be made without a top-to-bottom reinvention of government and society.

But a young public health worker had an idea. Stephen Luby had grown up in Omaha, Nebraska, where his father chaired the obstetrics and gynecology faculty at Creighton University. He attended medical school at the University of Texas Southwestern. But for some reason he was always drawn to public health work. He took a CDC job investigating infectious outbreaks in South Carolina, but when a position came open in the CDC's Pakistan office he jumped to take it. He arrived in Karachi with his schoolteacher wife and began publishing his first investigations of conditions there in the late nineties.

I had spoken to him once about how he thought through the difficulties. "If we had the kinds of water and sewage systems we've got in Omaha, we could solve these problems," he said. "But you have to wait decades for major infrastructure projects." So instead, he said, he looked for low-tech solutions. In this case, the solution he came up with was so humble it seemed laughable to his colleagues. It was soap.

Luby learned that Procter & Gamble, the consumer product conglomerate, was eager to prove the value of its new antibacterial Safeguard soap. So despite his colleagues' skepticism, he persuaded the company to provide a grant for a proper study and to supply cases of Safeguard both with and without triclocarban, an antibacterial agent. Once a week, field-workers from HOPE fanned out through twenty-five randomly chosen neighborhoods in the Karachi slums distributing the soap, some with the antibacterial agent and some without. They encouraged people to use it in six situations: to wash their bodies once daily and to wash their hands every time they defecated, wiped an infant, or were about to eat, prepare food, or feed it to others. The field-workers then collected information on illness rates among children in the test neighborhoods, as well as in eleven control neighborhoods, where no soap was distributed.

Luby and his team reported their results in a landmark paper published in the *Lancet* in 2005. Families in the test neighborhoods received an average of 3.3 bars of soap per week for one year. During this period, the incidence of diarrhea among children in these neighborhoods fell 52 percent compared to that in the control group, no matter which soap was used. The incidence of pneumonia fell 48 percent. And the incidence of impetigo, a bacterial skin infection, fell 35 percent. These were stunning results.

And they were achieved despite the illiteracy, the poverty, the crowding, and even the fact that, however much soap they used, people were still drinking and washing with contaminated water.

Ironically, Luby said, Procter & Gamble considered the study something of a disappointment. His research team had found no added benefit from having the antibacterial agent in the soap. Plain soap proved just as effective. Against seemingly insuperable odds, it was more than good enough. Plain soap was leverage.

The secret, he pointed out to me, was that the soap was more than soap. It was a behavior-change delivery vehicle. The researchers hadn't just handed out Safeguard, after all. They also gave out instructions—on leaflets and in person—explaining the six situations in which people should use it. This was essential to the difference they made. When one looks closely at the details of the Karachi study, one finds a striking statistic about the households in both the test and the control neighborhoods: At the start of the study, the average number of bars of soap households used was not zero. It was two bars per week. In other words, *they already had soap.*

So what did the study really change? Well, two things, Luby told me. First, "We removed the economic restraint on purchasing soap. People say soap is cheap and most households have soap. But we wanted people to wash a lot. And people are quite poor. So we removed that as a barrier." Second, and just as important, the project managed to make soap use more systematic.

Luby and his team had studied washing behavior in Pakistan, Bangladesh, and other locations around South Asia, and they found that almost everyone washes their hands after defecation. "There are strong ideas about purity in South Asia," he said. Even when the place to wash is far away, people go and clean their hands over 80 percent of the time, a rate that would put most denizens of airport bathrooms to shame. But the washing was not very effective, the researchers found. Often people did it too quickly. Or they cleaned just the "involved" hand. Or they used ash or mud rather than soap and water.

The soap experiment changed that. The field-workers gave specific instructions on hand-washing technique—on the need to wet both hands completely, to lather well, to rinse all the soap off, even if, out of necessity, as the published report noted, "hands were typically dried on participants' clothing." The instructions also got people used to washing at moments when they weren't used to doing so. "Before preparing food or feeding a child is not a time when people think about washing," Luby explained. The soap itself was also a factor. "It was really nice soap," he pointed out. It smelled good and lathered better than the usual soap people bought. People liked washing with it. "Global multinational corporations are really focused on having a good consumer experience, which sometimes public health people are not." Lastly, people liked receiving the soap. The public health field-workers were bringing them a gift rather than wagging a finger. And with the gift came a few basic ideas that would improve their lives and massively reduce disease.

Thinking back on the experiment, I was fascinated to realize that it was as much a checklist study as a soap study. So I wondered: Could a checklist be our soap for surgical care—simple, cheap, effective, and transmissible? I still had a hard time grasping how to make a checklist that could be both simple and effective for the manifold problems posed by surgery on a global scale. I was uncertain that it was even possible. But several of my colleagues were more sanguine when the idea was raised at the Geneva meeting.

One brought up the experience of Columbus Children's Hospital, which had developed a checklist to reduce surgical infections. Infection is one of the most common complications of surgery in children. And the most effective way to prevent it, aside from using proper antiseptic technique, is to make sure you give an appropriate antibiotic during the sixty-minute window before the incision is made.

The timing is key. Once the incision is made, it is too late for the antibiotic. Give it more than sixty minutes before the procedure, and the antibiotic has worn off. But give it on time and studies show this single step reduces the infection risk by up to half. Even if the antibiotic is squeezed into the bloodstream only thirty seconds before the incision is made, researchers have found, the circulation time is fast enough for the drug to reach the tissue before the knife breaches the skin.

Yet the step is commonly missed. In 2005, Columbus Children's Hospital examined its records and found that more than one-third of its appendectomy patients failed to get the right antibiotic at the right time. Some got it too soon. Some got it too late. Some did not receive an antibiotic at all.

It seems dumb. How hard could this be? Even people in medicine assume we get this kind of simple task right 100 percent of the time. But in fact we don't. With all the flurry of things that go on when a patient is wheeled into an operating room, this is exactly the sort of step that can be neglected. The anesthesiologists are the ones who have to provide the antibiotic, but they are concentrating on getting the patient safely and calmly to sleep—and this is no small matter when that patient is a scared eight-year-old lying naked on a cold table in a room full of strangers getting ready to cut into her. Add in an equipment malfunction ("Is that red light supposed to be blinking like that?"), or the patient's asthma acting up, or a page for the surgeon to call the emergency room, and you begin to see how something as mundane as an antibiotic can slip past.

The hospital's director of surgical administration, who happened to be not only a pediatric cardiac surgeon but also a pilot, decided to take the aviation approach. He designed a preincision "Cleared for Takeoff" checklist that he put on a whiteboard in each of the operating rooms. It was really simple. There was a check box for the nurse to verbally confirm with the team that they had the correct patient and the correct side of the body planned for surgery—something teams are supposed to verify in any case. And there was a further check box to confirm that the antibiotics were given (or else judged unnecessary, which they can be for some operations).

There wasn't much more to it. But getting teams to stop and use the checklist—to make it their habit—was clearly tricky. A couple of check boxes weren't going to do much all by themselves. So the surgical director gave some lectures to the nurses, anesthesiologists, and surgeons explaining what this checklist thing was all about. He also did something curious: he designed a little metal tent stenciled with the phrase *Cleared for Takeoff* and arranged for it to be placed in the surgical instrument kits. The metal tent was six inches long, just long enough to cover a scalpel, and the nurses were asked to set it over the scalpel when laying out the instruments before a case. This served as a reminder to run the checklist before making the incision. Just as important, it also made clear that the surgeon could not start the operation until the nurse gave the okay and removed the tent, a subtle cultural shift. Even a modest checklist had the effect of distributing power.

The surgical director measured the effect on care. After three months, 89 percent of appendicitis patients got the right antibiotic at the right time. After ten months, 100 percent did. The checklist had become habitual—and it had also become clear that team members could hold up an operation until the necessary steps were completed.

I was intrigued. But I remained doubtful. Yes, using a checklist, this one hospital got one aspect of care to go consistently right for surgical patients. I was even willing to believe their surgical infection rates had fallen significantly as a result. But to take a serious bite out of overall complication rates, I argued, we needed an approach that would help across the much wider range of ways in which surgery can go wrong.

Then Richard Reznick, the chairman of surgery at the University of Toronto, spoke up. He explained that his hospital had completed a feasibility trial using a much broader, twenty-one-item surgical checklist. They had tried to design it, he said, to catch a whole span of potential errors in surgical care. Their checklist had staff verbally confirm with one another that antibiotics had been given, that blood was available if required, that critical scans and test results needed for the operation were on hand, that any special instruments required were ready, and so on.

The checklist also included what they called a "team briefing." The team members were supposed to stop and take a moment simply to talk with one another before proceeding—about how long the surgeon expected the operation to take, how much blood loss everyone should be prepared for, whether the patient had any risks or concerns the team should know about.

Reznick had never heard about the demise of Master Builders, but he had gravitated intuitively toward the skyscraper solution— a mix of task and communication checks to manage the problem of proliferating complexity—and so had others, it turned out. A Johns Hopkins pancreatic surgeon named Martin Makary showed us an eighteen-item checklist that he'd tested with eleven surgeons for five months at his hospital. Likewise, a group of Southern California hospitals within the Kaiser health care system had studied a thirty-item "surgery preflight checklist" that actually predated the Toronto and Hopkins innovations. All of them followed the same basic design.

Surgery has, essentially, four big killers wherever it is done in the world: infection, bleeding, unsafe anesthesia, and what can only be called the unexpected. For the first three, science and experience have given us some straightforward and valuable preventive measures we think we consistently follow but don't. These misses are simple failures—perfect for a classic checklist. And as a result, all the researchers' checklists included precisely specified steps to catch them.

But the fourth killer—the unexpected—is an entirely different kind of failure, one that stems from the fundamentally complex risks entailed by opening up a person's body and trying to tinker with it. Independently, each of the researchers seemed to have realized that no one checklist could anticipate all the pitfalls a team must guard against. So they had determined that the most promising thing to do was just to have people stop and talk through the case together—to be ready as a team to identify and address each patient's unique, potentially critical dangers.

Perhaps all this seems kind of obvious. But it represents a significant departure from the way operations are usually conducted. Traditionally, surgery has been regarded as an individual performance—the surgeon as virtuoso, like a concert pianist. There's a reason that much of the world uses the phrase *operating theater*. The OR is the surgeon's stage. The surgeon strides under the lights and expects to start, everyone in their places, the patient laid out asleep and ready to go.

We surgeons want to believe that we've evolved along with the complexity of surgery, that we work more as teams now. But however embarrassing it may be for us to admit, researchers have observed that team members are commonly not all aware of a given patient's risks, or the problems they need to be ready for, or why the surgeon is doing the operation. In one survey of three hundred staff members as they exited the operating room following a case, one out of eight reported that they were not even sure about where the incision would be until the operation started.

Brian Sexton, a pioneering Johns Hopkins psychologist, has conducted a number of studies that provide a stark measure of how far we are from really performing as teams in surgery. In one, he surveyed more than a thousand operating room staff members from hospitals in five countries—the United States, Germany, Israel, Italy, and Switzerland—and found that although 64 percent of the surgeons rated their operations as having high levels of teamwork, just 39 percent of anesthesiologists, 28 percent of nurses, and 10 percent of anesthesia residents did. Not coincidentally, Sexton also found that one in four surgeons believed that junior team members should not question the decisions of a senior practitioner.

The most common obstacle to effective teams, it turns out, is not the occasional fire-breathing, scalpel-flinging, terror-inducing surgeon, though some do exist. (One favorite example: Several years ago, when I was in training, a senior surgeon grew incensed with one of my fellow residents for questioning the operative plan and commanded him to leave the table and stand in the corner until he was sorry. When he refused, the surgeon threw him out of the room and tried to get him suspended for insubordination.) No, the more familiar and widely dangerous issue is a kind of silent disengagement, the consequence of specialized technicians sticking narrowly to their domains. "That's not my problem" is possibly the worst thing people can think, whether they are start-ing an operation, taxiing an airplane full of passengers down a runway, or building a thousand-foot-tall skyscraper. But in medi-cine, we see it all the time. I've seen it in my own operating room.

Teamwork may just be hard in certain lines of work. Under conditions of extreme complexity, we inevitably rely on a divi-sion of tasks and expertise—in the operating room, for example, there is the surgeon, the surgical assistant, the scrub nurse, the circulating nurse, the anesthesiologist, and so on. They can each be technical masters at what they do. That's what we train them to be, and that alone can take years. But the evidence suggests we need them to see their job not just as performing their isolated set of tasks well but also as helping the group get the best possi-ble results. This requires finding a way to ensure that the group lets nothing fall between the cracks and also adapts as a team to whatever problems might arise.

I had assumed that achieving this kind of teamwork was

mostly a matter of luck. I'd certainly experienced it at times—difficult operations in which everyone was nonetheless firing on all cylinders, acting as one. I remember an eighty-year-old patient who required an emergency operation. He had undergone heart surgery the week before and had been recovering nicely. But during the night he'd developed a sudden, sharp, unrelenting pain in his abdomen, and over the course of the morning it had mounted steadily in severity. I was asked to see him from general surgery. I found him lying in bed, prostrate with pain. His heart rate was over one hundred and irregular. His blood pressure was dropping. And wherever I touched his abdomen, the sensation made him almost leap off the bed in agony.

He knew this was trouble. His mind was completely sharp. But he didn't seem scared.

"What do we need to do?" he asked between gritted teeth.

I explained that I believed his body had thrown a clot into his intestine's arterial supply. It was as if he'd had a stroke, only this one had cut off blood flow to his bowel, not his brain. Without blood flow, his bowel would turn gangrenous and rupture. This was not survivable without surgery. But, I also had to tell him, it was often not survivable even with surgery. Perhaps half of the patients in his circumstance make it through. If he was one of them, there would be many complications to worry about. He might need a ventilator or a feeding tube. He'd already been through one major operation. He was weak and not young. I asked him if he wanted to go ahead.

Yes, he said, but he wanted me to speak with his wife and son first. I reached them by phone. They too said to proceed. I called the operating room control desk and explained the situation. I needed an OR and a team right away. I'd take whatever and who-ever were available.

We got him to the OR within the hour. And as people assem-bled and set to work, there was the sense of a genuine team tak-ing form. Jay, the circulating nurse, introduced himself to the patient and briefly explained what everyone was doing. Steve, the scrub nurse, was already gowned and gloved, standing by with the sterile instruments at the ready. Zhi, the senior anesthesiolo-gist, and Thor, his resident, were conferring, making sure they had their plans straight, as they set out their drugs and equipment. Joaquim, the surgery resident, stood by with a Foley catheter, ready to slip it into the patient's bladder as soon as he was asleep.

The clock was ticking. The longer we took, the more bowel would die. The more bowel that died, the sicker the man would become and the lower his chance of survival. Everyone under-stood this, which by itself was a lot. People don't always get it—really feel the urgency of the patient's condition. But these people did. They were swift, methodical, and in sync. The case was far from easy, but for whatever reason, it seemed like nothing could thwart us.

The patient was a big man with a short neck and not much lung reserve, making it potentially difficult to place a breathing tube when Zhi sent him off to sleep. But Zhi had warned us of the possibility of trouble and everyone was ready with a backup plan and the instruments he and Thor might need. When Joaquim and I opened up the patient, we found that the right colon was black with gangrene—it had died—but it had not rup-tured, and the remaining three-fourths of the colon and all the small bowel seemed to be okay. This was actually good news.

The problem was limited. As we began removing the right colon, however, it became evident that the rest of the colon was not, in fact, in good shape. Where it should have been healthy pink, we found scattered dime- and quarter-sized patches of purple. The blood clots that had blocked off the main artery to the right colon had also showered into the arterial branches of the left side. We would have to remove the patient's entire colon, all four feet of it, and give him an ostomy—a bag for his excreted wastes. Steve, thinking ahead, asked Jay to grab a retractor we'd need. Joaquim nudged me to make the abdominal incision bigger, and he stayed with me at every step, clamping, cutting, and tying as we proceeded inch by inch through the blood vessels tethering the patient's colon. The patient began oozing blood from every raw surface—toxins from the gangrene were causing him to lose his ability to clot. But Zhi and Thor kept up with the fluid requirements and the patient's blood pressure was actually better halfway through than it had been at the beginning. When I mentioned that I thought the patient would need an ICU, Zhi told me he'd already arranged it and briefed the intensivist.

Because we'd worked as a single unit, not as separate technicians, the man survived. We were done with the operation in little more than two hours; his vital signs were stable; and he would leave the hospital just a few days later. The family gave me the credit, and I wish I could have taken it. But the operation had been symphonic, a thing of orchestral beauty.

Perhaps I could claim that the teamwork itself had been my doing. But its origins were mysterious to me. I'd have said it was just the good fortune of the circumstances—the accidental result of the individuals who happened to be available for the case and their particular chemistry on that particular afternoon. Although I operated with Zhi frequently, I hadn't worked with Jay or Steve in months, Joaquim in even longer. I'd worked with Thor just once. As a group of six, we'd never before done an operation together. Such a situation is not uncommon in hospitals of any significant size. My hospital has forty-two operating rooms, staffed by more than a thousand personnel. We have new nurses, technicians, residents, and physician staff almost constantly. We're virtually always adding strangers to our teams. As a consequence, the level of teamwork—an unspoken but critical component of success in surgery—is unpredictable. Yet somehow, from the moment we six were all dropped together into this particular case, things clicked. It had been almost criminally enjoyable.

This seemed like luck, as I say. But suppose it wasn't. That's what the checklists from Toronto and Hopkins and Kaiser raised as a possibility. Their insistence that people talk to one another about each case, at least just for a minute before starting, was basically a strategy to foster teamwork—a kind of team huddle, as it were. So was another step that these checklists employed, one that was quite unusual in my experience: surgical staff members were expected to stop and make sure that everyone knew one another's names.

The Johns Hopkins checklist spelled this out most explicitly. Before starting an operation with a new team, there was a check to ensure everyone introduced themselves by name and role: "I'm Atul Gawande, the attending surgeon"; "I'm Jay Powers, the circulating nurse"; "I'm Zhi Xiong, the anesthesiologist"—that sort of thing.

It felt kind of hokey to me, and I wondered how much

difference this step could really make. But it turned out to have been carefully devised. There have been psychology studies in various fields backing up what should have been self-evident—people who don't know one another's names don't work together nearly as well as those who do. And Brian Sexton, the Johns Hopkins psychologist, had done studies showing the same in operating rooms. In one, he and his research team buttonholed surgical staff members outside their operating rooms and asked them two questions: how would they rate the level of communications during the operation they had just finished and what were the names of the other staff members on the team? The researchers learned that about half the time the staff did not know one another's names. When they did, however, the communications ratings jumped significantly.

The investigators at Johns Hopkins and elsewhere had also observed that when nurses were given a chance to say their names and mention concerns at the beginning of a case, they were more likely to note problems and offer solutions. The researchers called it an "activation phenomenon." Giving people a chance to say something at the start seemed to activate their sense of participation and responsibility and their willingness to speak up.

These were limited studies and hardly definitive. But the initial results were enticing. Nothing had ever been shown to improve the ability of surgeons to broadly reduce harm to patients aside from experience and specialized training. Yet here, in three separate cities, teams had tried out these unusual checklists, and each had found a positive effect.

At Johns Hopkins, researchers specifically measured their checklist's effect on teamwork. Eleven surgeons had agreed to try it in their cases—seven general surgeons, two plastic surgeons, and two neurosurgeons. After three months, the number of team members in their operations reporting that they "functioned as a well-coordinated team" leapt from 68 percent to 92 percent.

At the Kaiser hospitals in Southern California, researchers had tested their checklist for six months in thirty-five hundred operations. During that time, they found that their staff's average rating of the teamwork climate improved from "good" to "outstanding." Employee satisfaction rose 19 percent. The rate of OR nurse turnover—the proportion leaving their jobs each year—dropped from 23 percent to 7 percent. And the checklist appeared to have caught numerous near errors. In one instance, the preoperative briefing led the team to recognize that a vial of potassium chloride had been switched with an antibiotic vial—a potentially lethal mix-up. In another, the checklist led the staff to catch a paperwork error that had them planning for a thoracotomy, an open-chest procedure with a huge front-to-back wound, when what the patient had come in for was actually a thoracoscopy, a videoscope procedure done through a quarter-inch incision.

At Toronto, the researchers physically observed operations for specific evidence of impact. They watched their checklist in use in only eighteen operations. But in ten of those eighteen, they found that it had revealed significant problems or ambiguities—in more than one case, a failure to give antibiotics, for example; in another, uncertainty about whether blood was available; and in several, the kinds of unique and individual patient problems that I would not have expected a checklist to help catch.

They reported one case, for example, involving an abdominal operation under a spinal anesthetic. In such procedures, we need the patient to report if he or she begins to feel even a slight twinge of pain, indicating the anesthetic might be wearing off and require supplementation. But this particular patient had a severe neurological condition that had left him unable to communicate verbally. Instead, he communicated through hand signals. Normally, we restrain the arms and hands of patients to keep them from inadvertently reaching around the sterile drapes and touching the surgeons or the operative field. In this instance, however, the regular routine would have caused a serious problem, but this was not clearly recognized by the team until just before the incision was made. That was when the surgeon walked in, pulled on his gown and gloves, and stepped up to the operating table. Because of the checklist, instead of taking the knife, he paused and conferred with everyone about the plans for the operation. The Toronto report included a transcript of the discussion.

"Are there any special anesthetic considerations?" the surgeon asked.

"Just his dysarthria," the anesthesiologist said, referring to the patient's inability to speak.

The surgeon thought for a moment. "It may be difficult to gauge his neurological function because we have these issues," he said.

The anesthesiologist agreed. "I've worked out a system of hand signals with him."

"His arm will [need to] be accessible then—not tucked," the surgeon said. The anesthesiologist nodded, and the team then worked out a way to leave the patient's arms free but protected from reaching around or beneath the drapes.

"My other concern is the number of people in the room," the

anesthesiologist went on, "because noise and movement may interfere with our ability to communicate with the patient."

"We can request silence," the surgeon said. Problem solved.

None of these studies was complete enough to prove that a surgical checklist could produce what WHO was ultimately looking for—a measurable, inexpensive, and substantial reduction in overall complications from surgery. But by the end of the Geneva conference, we had agreed that a safe surgery checklist was worth testing on a larger scale.

A working group took the different checklists that had been tried and condensed them into a single one. It had three "pause points," as they are called in aviation—three points at which the team must stop to run through a set of checks before proceeding. There was a pause right before the patient is given anesthesia, one after the patient is anesthetized but before the incision is made, and one at the end of the operation, before the patient is wheeled out of the operating room. The working group members divvied up the myriad checks for allergies, antibiotics, anesthesia equipment, and so on among the different pause points. They added any other checks they could think of that might make a difference in care. And they incorporated the communication checks in which everyone in the operating room ensures that they know one another's names and has a chance to weigh in on critical plans and concerns.

We made a decision to set up a proper pilot study of our safe surgery checklist in a range of hospitals around the world, for which WHO committed to providing the funds. I was thrilled and optimistic. When I returned home to Boston, I jumped to give the checklist a try myself. I printed it out and took it to the operating room. I told the nurses and anesthesiologists what I'd learned in Geneva.

"So how about we try this awesome checklist?" I said. It detailed steps for everything from equipment inspection to antibiotic administration to the discussions we should have. The rest of the team eyed me skeptically, but they went along. "Sure, whatever you say." This was not the first time I'd cooked up some cockamamie idea.

I gave the checklist to Dee, the circulating nurse, and asked her to run through the first section with us at the right time. Fifteen minutes later, we were about to put the patient to sleep under general anesthesia, and I had to say, Wait, what about the checklist?

"I already did it," Dee said. She showed me the sheet. All the boxes were checked off.

No, no, no, I said. It's supposed to be a *verbal* checklist, a *team* checklist.

"Where does it say that?" she asked. I looked again. She was right. It didn't say that anywhere.

Just try it verbally anyway, I said.

Dee shrugged and started going through the list. But some of the checks were ambiguous. Was she supposed to confirm that everyone knew the patient's allergies or actually state the allergies? she asked. And after a few minutes of puzzling our way through the list, everyone was becoming exasperated. Even the patient started shifting around on the table.

"Is everything okay?" she asked.

Oh yes, I told her. We're only going through our checklist. Don't worry.

But I was getting impatient, too. The checklist was too long. It was unclear. And past a certain point, it was starting to feel like a distraction from the person we had on the table.

By the end of the day, we had stopped using the checklist. Forget making this work around the world. It wasn't even working in one operating room.

6. THE CHECKLIST FACTORY

Some time after that first miserable try, I did what I should have done to begin with. I went to the library and pulled out a few articles on how flight checklists are made. As great as the construction-world checklists seemed to be, they were employed in projects that routinely take months to complete. In surgery, minutes matter. The problem of time seemed a serious limitation. But aviation had this challenge, too, and somehow pilots' checklists met it.

Among the articles I found was one by Daniel Boorman from the Boeing Company in Seattle, Washington. I gave him a call. He proved to be a veteran pilot who'd spent the last two decades developing checklists and flight deck controls for Boeing aircraft from the 747-400 forward. He'd most recently been one of the technical leaders behind the flight deck design for the new 787

Dreamliner, including its pilot controls, displays, and system of checklists. He is among the keepers of what could be called Boeing's "flight philosophy." When you get on a Boeing aircraft, there is a theory that governs the way your cockpit crew flies that plane—what their routines are, what they do manually, what they leave to computers, and how they should react when the unexpected occurs. Few have had more experience translating the theory into practice than Dan Boorman. He is the lineal descendant of the pilots who came up with that first checklist for the B-17 bomber three-quarters of a century ago. He has studied thousands of crashes and near crashes over the years, and he has made a science of averting human error.

I had a trip to Seattle coming up, and he was kind enough to agree to a visit. So one fall day, I drove a rental car down a long flat road on the city's outskirts to Boeing's headquarters. They appeared rather ordinary—a warren of low, rectangular, institutional-looking buildings that would not be out of place on the campus of an underfunded state college, except for the tarmac and hangar of airplanes behind them. Boorman came out to meet me at security. He was fifty-one, pilot-trim, in slacks and an open-collared oxford shirt—more like an engineering professor than a company man. He took me along a path of covered concrete sidewalks to Building 3-800, which was as plain and functional as it sounds. A dusty display case with yellowing pictures of guys in silver flight suits appeared not to have been touched since the 1960s. The flight test division was a fluorescent-lit space filled with dun-colored cubicles. We sat down in a windowless conference room in their midst. Piles of checklist handbooks from US Airways, Delta, United, and other airlines lay stacked against a wall.

Boorman showed me one of the handbooks. It was spiral

bound, about two hundred pages long, with numerous yellow tabs. The aviation checklist had clearly evolved since the days of a single card for taxi, takeoff, and landing, and I wondered how anyone could actually use this hefty volume. As he walked me through it, however, I realized the handbook was comprised not of one checklist but of scores of them. Each one was remarkably brief, usually just a few lines on a page in big, easy-to-read type. And each applied to a different situation. Taken together, they covered a vast range of flight scenarios.

First came what pilots call their "normal" checklists—the routine lists they use for everyday aircraft operations. There were the checks they do before starting the engines, before pulling away from the gate, before taxiing to the runway, and so on. In all, these took up just three pages. The rest of the handbook consisted of the "non-normal" checklists covering every conceivable emergency situation a pilot might run into: smoke in the cockpit, different warning lights turning on, a dead radio, a copilot becoming disabled, and engine failure, to name just a few. They addressed situations most pilots never encounter in their entire careers. But the checklists were there should they need them.

Boorman showed me the one for when the DOOR FWD CARGO warning light goes on in midflight. This signals that the forward cargo door is not closed and secure, which is extremely dangerous. He told me of a 1989 case he'd studied in which exactly this problem occurred. An electrical short had caused a Boeing 747 cargo door to become unlatched during a United Airlines flight out of Honolulu on its way to Auckland, New Zealand, with 337 passengers on board. The plane was climbing past twenty-two thousand feet and the cabin was pressurized to maintain oxygen levels for the passengers. At that altitude, a loose, unlatched cargo door is a serious hazard: if it opens enough to begin leaking air, the large pressure difference between inside and out causes a "ring-pull" effect—an explosive release like pulling the ring top on a shaken soda can. In the Honolulu flight, the explosion blew out the cargo door almost instantly and took with it several upper-deck windows and five rows of business class seats. Nine passengers were lost at sea. Passengers in adjacent seats were held in only by their seat belts. A flight attendant in the aisle was nearly sucked out, too, but an alert passenger managed to grab her ankle and pin her down, inches from the gaping hole.

The crew had had no time to prevent the catastrophe. From unlatching to blowout and the loss of nine lives took no more than 1.5 seconds. Boeing subsequently redesigned the electrical system for its cargo doors and—because no latch is foolproof—installed extra latches, as well. If one fails, the DOOR FWD CARGO light goes on and the crew has more time to respond. There is a window of opportunity to stop a blowout. That's where the checklist comes in.

When a latch gives way, Boorman explained, a crew should not tinker with the door or trust that the other latches will hold. Instead, the key is to equalize the difference between inside and outside pressures. The more you lower the cabin pressure, the less likely the door will explode away.

Airplanes have an easy way to lower the pressure, apparently: you hit an emergency override switch that vents the cabin air and releases the pressurization in about thirty seconds. This solution is problematic, however. First, the sudden loss of pressure can be extremely uncomfortable for passengers, particularly given the ear pain it causes. Infants fare the worst, as their eustachian tubes haven't developed sufficiently to adjust to the change. Second, depressurizing a plane at an altitude of twenty or thirty thousand feet is like dropping passengers onto the summit of Mount Everest. The air is too thin to supply enough oxygen for the body and brain.

The United Airlines flight offered a vivid lesson in what could happen, for the cargo door blowout instantly depressurized the plane, and once the initial, explosive decompression was over, lack of oxygen became the prime danger for the passengers and crew. Getting sucked into the void was no longer the issue. Everyone was able to stay well away from the ten-by-fifteen-foot hole. The temperature, however, plummeted to near freezing, and the oxygen levels fell so low that the crew became light-headed and feared losing consciousness. Sensors automatically dropped oxygen masks, but the oxygen supply on airplanes is expected to last only ten minutes. Moreover, the supply might not even work, which is exactly what happened on that flight.

The cockpit voice recorder caught the events from the moment the cargo door blew away:

CAPTAIN: What the [expletive] was that?
FIRST OFFICER: I don't know.

The pilots notified flight control that something had gone wrong. Two seconds later, their cabin pressure and oxygen levels were gone.

FIRST OFFICER: Put your mask on, Dave.
CAPTAIN: Yeah.
FIRST OFFICER: Honolulu Center Continental One Heavy, did you want us to turn left did you say?

RADIO: Continental One Heavy affirmative.

FIRST OFFICER: Turning now.

CAPTAIN: I can't get any oxygen.

FLIGHT ENGINEER: What do you want me to do now?

VOICE UNIDENTIFIED: [expletive]

FIRST OFFICER: You okay?

CAPTAIN: Yeah.

FIRST OFFICER: Are you getting oxygen? We're not getting any oxygen.

FLIGHT ENGINEER: No I'm not getting oxygen either.

The blast had torn out the oxygen supply lines, an investigation later found. Only by luck did the cockpit crew maintain enough control of the plane to descend to an altitude with sufficient oxygen levels. The pilots were then able to turn back to the Honolulu airport. All eighteen crew and 328 terrified remaining passengers survived.

The lesson for pilots is complicated. If you're jetting along at thirty thousand feet and the DOOR FWD CARGO warning light goes on, yes, eliminating the pressure differential between inside and outside to stop the door from blowing out is a very good idea, but doing it by hitting the emergency depressurization switch and leaving everyone short of oxygen is not. Instead, Boorman said, the best thing to do is to make a rapid but controlled descent to eight thousand feet or as close to it as possible. At that height, you can safely release the plane's inside pressure— the oxygen levels at eight thousand feet are adequate for people to breathe. (It is the altitude of Aspen, Colorado, after all.) And with that, the risk of a United Airlines–style door blowout will be safely eliminated.

The DOOR FWD CARGO checklist spelled out all these steps. And Boorman stressed how carefully it was designed for a crew to use in an emergency. All of Boeing's aviation checklists—the company issues over one hundred per year, either new or revised—are put together meticulously. Boorman's flight operations group is a checklist factory, and the experts in it have learned a thing or two over the years about how to make the lists work.

There are good checklists and bad, Boorman explained. Bad checklists are vague and imprecise. They are too long; they are hard to use; they are impractical. They are made by desk jockeys with no awareness of the situations in which they are to be deployed. They treat the people using the tools as dumb and try to spell out every single step. They turn people's brains off rather than turn them on.

Good checklists, on the other hand, are precise. They are efficient, to the point, and easy to use even in the most difficult situations. They do not try to spell out everything—a checklist cannot fly a plane. Instead, they provide reminders of only the most critical and important steps—the ones that even the highly skilled professionals using them could miss. Good checklists are, above all, practical.

The power of checklists is limited, Boorman emphasized. They can help experts remember how to manage a complex process or configure a complex machine. They can make priorities clearer and prompt people to function better as a team. By themselves, however, checklists cannot make anyone follow them.

I could imagine, for instance, that when the DOOR FWD CARGO warning light goes on in a cockpit, a pilot's first instinct might not be to grab the checklist book. How many times, after all, does a flashing warning light end up being a false alarm? The flight would likely have been going smoothly. No noises. No explosion. No strange thud. Just this pesky light flipping on. The ground crew already inspected the doors at the preflight check and found no problem. Besides, only 1 in 500,000 flights ever suffers an accident of any kind. So a person could be tempted to troubleshoot—maybe have someone check the circuitry before deciding that something might really have gone wrong.

Pilots nonetheless turn to their checklists for two reasons. First, they are trained to do so. They learn from the beginning of flight school that their memory and judgment are unreliable and that lives depend on their recognizing that fact. Second, the checklists have proved their worth—they work. However much pilots are taught to trust their procedures more than their instincts, that doesn't mean they will do so blindly. Aviation checklists are by no means perfect. Some have been found confusing or unclear or flawed. Nonetheless, they have earned pilots' faith. Face-to-face with catastrophe, they are astonishingly willing to turn to their checklists.

In the cockpit voice recorder transcript of the United flight from Honolulu, for example, the pilots' readiness to rely on procedure is striking. The circumstances were terrifying. Debris was flying. The noise was tremendous. Their hearts were probably racing. And they had a lot to focus on. Beyond the immediate oxygen problem, ejected sections of fuselage had flown into engine No. 3, on the right wing, and disabled it. Additional debris had hit engine No. 4 and set it on fire. The outer-edge wing flaps had been damaged. And sitting up front, trying to figure out what to do, the cockpit crew still had no idea what had really happened. They thought a bomb had gone off. They didn't know the full extent of the damage, or whether another blast might occur. They nonetheless needed to shut down the ruined engines, notify air traffic control of the emergency, descend to a safe altitude, determine how maneuverable the plane was, sort out which alarms on their instrument panel they could ignore and which ones they couldn't, and decide whether to ditch the plane in the ocean or return to Honolulu. The greatest test of where crew members place their trust—in their instincts or in their procedures—is how they handle such a disaster.

So what did they do? They grabbed their checklist book:

CAPTAIN: You want me to read a checklist?
FLIGHT ENGINEER: Yeah, I got it out. When you're ready.
CAPTAIN: Ready.

There was a lot to go through, and they had to make good choices about what procedures to turn to first. Following their protocols, they reduced their altitude, got the two damaged engines shut down safely, tested the plane's ability to land despite the wing damage, dumped fuel to lighten their load, and successfully returned to Honolulu.

To pilots, the checklists have proved worth trusting, and that is thanks to people like Boorman, who have learned how to make good checklists instead of bad. Clearly, our surgery checklist had a ways to go.

When you're making a checklist, Boorman explained, you have a number of key decisions. You must define a clear pause point at which the checklist is supposed to be used (unless the moment is obvious, like when a warning light goes on or an engine fails). You must decide whether you want a DO-CONFIRM checklist or a READ-DO checklist. With a DO-CONFIRM checklist, he said, team members perform their jobs from memory and experience, often separately. But then they stop. They pause to run the checklist and confirm that everything that was supposed to be done was done. With a READ-DO checklist, on the other hand, people carry out the tasks as they check them off—it's more like a recipe. So for any new checklist created from scratch, you have to pick the type that makes the most sense for the situation.

The checklist cannot be lengthy. A rule of thumb some use is to keep it to between five and nine items, which is the limit of working memory. Boorman didn't think one had to be religious on this point.

"It all depends on the context," he said. "In some situations you have only twenty seconds. In others, you may have several minutes."

But after about sixty to ninety seconds at a given pause point, the checklist often becomes a distraction from other things. People start "shortcutting." Steps get missed. So you want to keep the list short by focusing on what he called "the killer items"—the steps that are most dangerous to skip and sometimes overlooked nonetheless. (Data establishing which steps are most critical and how frequently people miss them are highly coveted in aviation, though not always available.)

The wording should be simple and exact, Boorman went on, and use the familiar language of the profession. Even the look of the checklist matters. Ideally, it should fit on one page. It should be free of clutter and unnecessary colors. It should use both uppercase and lowercase text for ease of reading. (He went so far as to recommend using a sans serif type like Helvetica.)

To some extent, we had covered this territory in drafting our surgery checklist. No question, it needed some trimming, and many items on the list could be sharper and less confusing. I figured we could fix it easily. But Boorman was adamant about one further point: no matter how careful we might be, no matter how much thought we might put in, a checklist has to be tested in the real world, which is inevitably more complicated than expected. First drafts always fall apart, he said, and one needs to study how, make changes, and keep testing until the checklist works consistently.

This is not easy to do in surgery, I pointed out. Not in aviation, either, he countered. You can't unlatch a cargo door in mid-flight and observe how a crew handles the consequences. But that's why they have flight simulators, and he offered to show me one.

I tried not to seem like a kid who'd just been offered a chance to go up to the front of the plane and see the cockpit. Sure, I said. That sounds neat.

A short stroll later, we entered an adjacent building, walked through an ordinary-looking metal door, and came upon a strange, boxlike space capsule. It was mounted on three massive hydraulic legs. We appeared to be on a platform of some kind, as the capsule was on our level and the legs went down to the floor below. Boorman led me into the thing and inside was a complete Boeing 777-200ER cockpit. He had me climb into the captain's seat on the left while he took the one on the right. He showed me how to belt myself in. The windshield was three black plasma screens, until an assistant turned them on.

"What airport do you want?" Boorman asked. "We've got almost every airport in the world loaded into the database."

I chose the Seattle-Tacoma airport, where I'd landed the day before, and suddenly the tarmac came up on the screens. It was amazing. We were parked at a gate. Guys with baggage carts whizzed back and forth in front of me. In the distance, I could see other airplanes taxiing in and out of their gates.

Boorman walked me through our checks. Built into the wall panel on my left was a slot for the checklist book, which I could grab at any time, but it was just a backup. Pilots usually use an electronic checklist that appears on the center console. He demonstrated how one goes through it, reading from the screen.

"Oxygen," he said and pointed to where I could confirm the supply.

"Tested, 100 percent," I was supposed to respond.

"Flight instruments," he said, and showed me where I could find the heading and altimeter readings.

On our initial cockpit check, we had just four preflight items to review. Before starting the engines, we had six more items, plus a prompt asking us to confirm that we'd completed our "taxi and takeoff briefing"—the discussion between pilot and copilot in which they talk through their taxi and takeoff plans and concerns. Boorman went through it with me.

His plan, as far as I could follow, was to do a "normal" takeoff on Runway 16L, lift off at a whole lot of knots per hour, "fly the standard departure" to the southeast, and climb to twenty thousand feet—I think. He also said something important sounding about the radio settings. Then he mentioned a bunch of crazy stuff—like if we had an engine failure during takeoff, we would power down if we were still on the ground, continue climbing if we had one engine left, or look for a good landing site nearby if we didn't. I nodded sagely.

"Do you have any concerns?" he asked.

"Nope," I said.

He started the engines, and although there were no actual engines, you could hear them rev up, and we had to talk louder to be heard above them. Before taxiing out to the runway, we paused again for five more checks: whether anti-icing was necessary and completed, the autobrakes were set, the flight controls were checked, the ground equipment was cleared, and no warning lights were on.

The three checklists took no time at all—maybe thirty seconds each—plus maybe a minute for the briefing. The brevity was no accident, Boorman said. People had spent hours watching pilots try out early versions in simulators, timing them, refining them, paring them down to their most efficient essentials.

When he was satisfied that we were ready, he had me pull out of the gate. I was supposed to be the pilot for this flight, believe it or not. He directed me to push the pedal brake down hard with two feet to release it. I felt a jolt as the plane lurched forward. I controlled the direction of the nose wheel with a tiller on my left—a spinning metal handle that I wound forward to turn right and backward to turn left—and the speed with the throttle controls, three levers in the center console. I weaved like a sot at first but got the hang of it by the time we reached the runway. I throttled back down to idle and locked the brake with both feet to wait our turn for takeoff. Boorman called up the Before Takeoff checklist.

"Flaps," he said.

"Set," I said.

This was getting to be fun. We got notification from the control tower that we were cleared. I unlocked the brakes, again. Boorman showed me how far to push the throttle. We began accelerating down the runway, slowly at first, and then it felt like we were rocketing. I pressed the right and left rudder pedals to try to keep us on the center line. Then, when he gave me the word, I pulled back on the yoke—what I'd thought of as the steering wheel—and felt the plane lift into the air. I don't know how the simulator does it, but it really did seem like we were airborne.

We rose into the clouds. I could see the city fall away below us. We slowly climbed to twenty thousand feet. And that was when the DOOR FWD CARGO light went on. I'd forgotten that this was the whole point of the exercise. The first couple lines of the electronic checklist came up on the screen, but I grabbed the paper one just so I could see the whole thing laid out.

It was, I noticed, a READ-DO checklist—read it and do it—with only seven lines. The page explained that the forward cargo door was not closed and secure and that our objective was to reduce the risk of door separation.

This was just a simulation, I knew perfectly well. But I still felt my pulse picking up. The checklist said to lower the cabin pressure *partially*. Actually, what it said was, "LDG ALT selector"—which Boorman showed me is the cabin pressure control on the overhead panel—"PULL ON and set to 8000." I did as instructed.

Next, the checklist said to descend to the lowest safe altitude or eight thousand feet, whichever is higher. I pushed forward on the yoke to bring the nose down. Boorman indicated the gauge to watch, and after a few minutes we leveled off at eight thousand feet. Now, the checklist said, put the air outflow switches on manual and push them in for thirty seconds to release the remaining pressure. I did this, too. And that was it. The plane didn't explode. We were safe. I wanted to give Boorman a high five. This flying thing is easy, I wanted to say.

There were, however, all kinds of steps that the checklist had not specified—notifying the radio control tower that we had an emergency, for example, briefing the flight attendants, determining the safest nearby airport to land and have the cargo door inspected. I hadn't done any of these yet. But Boorman had. The omissions were intentional, he explained. Although these are critical steps, experience had shown that professional pilots virtually never fail to perform them when necessary. So they didn't need to be on the checklist—and in fact, he argued, shouldn't be there.

It is common to misconceive how checklists function in complex lines of work. They are not comprehensive how-to guides, whether for building a skyscraper or getting a plane out of trouble. They are quick and simple tools aimed to buttress the skills of expert professionals. And by remaining swift and usable and resolutely modest, they are saving thousands upon thousands of lives.

One more aviation checklist story, this one relatively recent. The incident occurred on January 17, 2008, as British Airways Flight 38 approached London from Beijing after almost eleven hours in the air with 152 people aboard. The Boeing 777 was making its final descent into Heathrow airport. It was just past noon. Clouds were thin and scattered. Visibility was more than six miles. The wind was light, and the temperature was mild despite the season—50 degrees Fahrenheit. The flight had been completely uneventful to this point.

Then, at two miles from the airport, 720 feet over a residential neighborhood, just when the plane should have accelerated slightly to level off its descent, the engines gave out. First the right engine rolled back to minimal power, then the left. The copilot was at the controls for the landing, and however much he tried to increase thrust, he got nothing from the engines. For no apparent reason, the plane had gone eerily silent.

He extended the wing flaps to make the plane glide as much as possible and to try to hold it on its original line of approach. But the aircraft was losing forward speed too quickly. The plane had become a 350,000-pound stone falling out of the air. Crash investigators with Britain's Air Accidents Investigation Branch later determined that it was falling twenty-three feet per second. At impact, almost a quarter mile short of the runway, the plane was calculated to be moving at 124 miles per hour.

Only by sheer luck was no one killed, either on board or on the ground. The plane narrowly missed crashing through the roofs of nearby homes. Passengers in cars on the perimeter road around Heathrow saw the plane coming down and thought they were about to be killed. Through a coincidence of international significance, one of those cars was carrying British prime minister Gordon Brown to his plane for his first official visit to China. "It was just yards above our heads, almost skimming a lamppost as the plane came in very fast and very, very low," an aide traveling with the prime minister told London's *Daily Mirror*.

The aircraft hit a grassy field just beyond the perimeter road with what a witness described as "an enormous bang." The nose wheels collapsed on impact. The right main landing gear separated from the aircraft, and its two right front wheels broke away, struck the right rear fuselage, and penetrated through the passenger compartment at rows 29 and 30. The left main landing gear pushed up through the wing. Fourteen hundred liters of jet fuel came pouring out. Witnesses saw sparks, but somehow the fuel did not ignite. Although the aircraft was totaled by the blunt force of the crash, the passengers emerged mostly unharmed—the plane had gone into a thousand-foot ground slide that slowed its momentum and tempered the impact. Only a dozen or so passengers required hospitalization. The worst injury was a broken leg.

Investigators from the AAIB were on the scene within an hour trying to piece together what had happened. Their initial reports, published one month and then four months after the crash, were documents of frustration. They removed the engines, fuel system, and data recorders and took them apart piece by piece. Yet they found no engine defects whatsoever. The data download showed that the fuel flow to the engines had reduced for some reason, but inspection of the fuel feed lines with a boroscope—a long fiberoptic videoscope—showed no defects or obstructions. Tests of the valves and wiring that controlled fuel flow showed they had all functioned properly. The fuel tanks contained no debris that could have blocked the fuel lines.

Attention therefore turned to the fuel itself. Tests showed it to be normal Jet A-1 fuel. But investigators, considering the flight's path over the Arctic Circle, wondered: could the fuel have frozen in flight, caused the crash, then thawed before they could find a trace of it? The British Airways flight had followed a path through territory at the border of China and Mongolia where the recorded

ambient air temperature that midwinter day was −85 degrees
Fahrenheit. As the plane crossed the Ural Mountains and Scandi-
navia, the recorded temperature fell to −105 degrees. These were
not considered exceptional temperatures for polar flight.
Although the freezing point for Jet A-1 fuel is −53 degrees, the
dangers were thought to have been resolved. Aircraft taking Arctic routes are designed to protect the fuel against extreme cold,
and the pilots monitor the fuel temperature constantly. Cross-
polar routes for commercial aircraft opened in February 2001,
and thousands of planes have traveled them without incident
since. In fact, on the British Airways flight, the lowest fuel temperature recorded was −29 degrees, well above the fuel's freezing
point. Furthermore, the plane was over mild-weathered London,
not the Urals, when the engines lost power.

Nonetheless, investigators remained concerned that the
plane's flight path had played a role. They proposed an elabo-
rate theory. Jet fuel normally has a minor amount of water moisture in it, less than two drops per gallon. During cold-air flights,
the moisture routinely freezes and floats in the fuel as a suspension of tiny ice crystals. This had never been considered a significant problem. But maybe on a long, very smooth polar flight—as
this one was—the fuel flow becomes so slow that the crystals have
time to sediment and perhaps accumulate somewhere in the fuel
tank. Then, during a brief burst of acceleration, such as on the
final approach, the sudden increase in fuel flow might release the
accumulation, causing blockage of the fuel lines.

The investigators had no hard evidence for this idea. It
seemed a bit like finding a man suffocated in bed and arguing that
all the oxygen molecules had randomly jumped to the other end

of the room, leaving him to die in his sleep—possible, but preposterously unlikely. Nonetheless, the investigators tested what would happen if they injected water directly into the fuel system under freezing conditions. The crystals that formed, they found, could indeed clog the lines.

Almost eight months after the crash, this was all they had for an explanation. Everyone was anxious to do something before a similar accident occurred. Just in case the explanation was right, the investigators figured out some midflight maneuvers to fix the problem. When an engine loses power, a pilot's instinct is to increase the thrust—to rev the engine. But if ice crystals have accumulated, increasing the fuel flow only throws more crystals into the fuel lines. So the investigators determined that pilots should do the opposite and idle the engine momentarily. This reduces fuel flow and permits time for heat exchangers in the piping to melt the ice—it takes only seconds—allowing the engines to recover. At least that was the investigators' best guess.

So in September 2008, the Federal Aviation Administration in the United States issued a detailed advisory with new procedures pilots should follow to keep ice from accumulating on polar flights and also to recover flight control if icing nonetheless caused engine failure. Pilots across the world were somehow supposed to learn about these findings and smoothly incorporate them into their flight practices within thirty days. The remarkable thing about this episode—and the reason the story is worth telling—is that the pilots did so.

How this happened—it involved a checklist, of course—is instructive. But first think about what happens in most lines of professional work when a major failure occurs. To begin with, we rarely investigate our failures. Not in medicine, not in teaching, not in the legal profession, not in the financial world, not in virtually any other kind of work where the mistakes do not turn up on cable news. A single type of error can affect thousands, but because it usually touches only one person at a time, we tend not to search as hard for explanations.

Sometimes, though, failures are investigated. We learn better ways of doing things. And then what happens? Well, the findings might turn up in a course or a seminar, or they might make it into a professional journal or a textbook. In ideal circumstances, we issue some inch-thick set of guidelines or a declaration of standards. But getting the word out is far from assured, and incorporating the changes often takes years.

One study in medicine, for example, examined the aftermath of nine different major treatment discoveries such as the finding that the pneumococcus vaccine protects not only children but also adults from respiratory infections, one of our most common killers. On average, the study reported, it took doctors *seventeen years* to adopt the new treatments for at least half of American patients.

What experts like Dan Boorman have recognized is that the reason for the delay is not usually laziness or unwillingness. The reason is more often that the necessary knowledge has not been translated into a simple, usable, and systematic form. If the only thing people did in aviation was issue dense, pages-long bulletins for every new finding that might affect the safe operation of airplanes—well, it would be like subjecting pilots to the same deluge of almost 700,000 medical journal articles per year that clinicians must contend with. The information would be unmanageable.

But instead, when the crash investigators issued their

bulletin—as dense and detailed as anything we find in medicine—
Boorman and his team buckled down to the work of distilling
the information into its practical essence. They drafted a revision
to the standard checklists pilots use for polar flights. They sharp-
ened, trimmed, and puzzled over pause points—how are pilots to
know, for instance, whether an engine is failing because of icing
instead of something else? Then his group tested the checklist
with pilots in the simulator and found problems and fixed them
and tested again.

It took about two weeks for the Boeing team to complete the
testing and refinement, and then they had their checklist. They
sent it to every owner of a Boeing 777 in the world. Some airlines
used the checklist as it was, but many, if not most, went on to
make their own adjustments. Just as schools or hospitals tend to
do things slightly differently, so do airlines, and they are encouraged to modify the checklists to fit into their usual procedures.
(This customization is why, when airlines merge, among the
fiercest battles is the one between the pilots over whose checklists
will be used.) Within about a month of the recommendations
becoming available, pilots had the new checklist in their hands—
or in their cockpit computers. And they used it.

How do we know? Because on November 26, 2008, the disaster
almost happened again. This time it was a Delta Air Lines flight
from Shanghai to Atlanta with 247 people aboard. The Boeing 777
was at thirty-nine thousand feet over Great Falls, Montana, when it
experienced "an uncommanded rollback" of the right No. 2
engine—the engine, in other words, failed. Investigation later
showed that ice had blocked the fuel lines—the icing theory was
correct—and Boeing instituted a mechanical change to keep it
from happening again. But in the moment, the loss of one engine

in this way, potentially two, over the mountains of Montana could have been catastrophic.

The pilot and copilot knew what to do, though. They got out their checklist and followed the lessons it offered. Because they did, the engine recovered, and 247 people were saved. It went so smoothly, the passengers didn't even notice.

This, it seemed to me, was something to hope for in surgery.

7. THE TEST

Back in Boston, I set my research team to work making our fledgling surgery checklist more usable. We tried to follow the lessons from aviation. We made it clearer. We made it speedier. We adopted mainly a DO-CONFIRM rather than a READ-DO format, to give people greater flexibility in performing their tasks while nonetheless having them stop at key points to confirm that critical steps have not been overlooked. The checklist emerged vastly improved.

Next, we tested it in a simulator, otherwise known as the conference room on my hallway at the school of public health where I do research. We had an assistant lie on a table. She was our patient. We assigned different people to play the part of the surgeon, the surgical assistant, the nurses (one scrubbed-in and one circulating), and the anesthesiologist. But we hit problems just trying to get started.

Who, for example, was supposed to bring things to a halt and kick off the checklist? We'd been vague about that, but it proved no small decision. Getting everyone's attention in an operation requires a degree of assertiveness—a level of control—that only the surgeon routinely has. Perhaps, I suggested, the surgeon should get things started. I got booed for this idea. In aviation, there is a reason the "pilot not flying" starts the checklist, someone pointed out. The "pilot flying" can be distracted by flight tasks and liable to skip a checklist. Moreover, dispersing the responsibility sends the message that everyone—not just the captain—is responsible for the overall well-being of the flight and should have the power to question the process. If a surgery checklist was to make a difference, my colleagues argued, it needed to do likewise—to spread responsibility and the power to question. So we had the circulating nurse call the start.

Must nurses make written check marks? No, we decided, they didn't have to. This wasn't a record-keeping procedure. We were aiming for a team conversation to ensure that everyone had reviewed what was needed for the case to go as well as possible.

Every line of the checklist needed tweaking. We timed each successive version by a clock on the wall. We wanted the checks at each of the three pause points—before anesthesia, before incision, and before leaving the OR—to take no more than about sixty seconds, and we weren't there yet. If we wanted acceptance in the high-pressure environment of operating rooms, the checklist had to be swift to use. We would have to cut some lines, we realized—the non–killer items.

This proved the most difficult part of the exercise. An inherent tension exists between brevity and effectiveness. Cut too much and you won't have enough checks to improve care. Leave too much in and the list becomes too long to use. Furthermore, an item critical to one expert might not be critical to another. In the spring of 2007, we reconvened our WHO group of international experts in London to consider these questions. Not surprisingly, the most intense disagreements flared over what should stay in and what should come out.

European and American studies had discovered, for example, that in long operations teams could substantially reduce patients' risks of developing deep venous thrombosis—blood clots in their legs that can travel to their lungs with fatal consequences—by injecting a low dose of a blood thinner, such as heparin, or slipping compression stockings onto their legs. But researchers in China and India dispute the necessity, as they have reported far lower rates of blood clots in their populations than in the West and almost no deaths. Moreover, for poor- and middle-income countries, the remedies—stockings or heparin—aren't cheap. And even a slight mistake by inexperienced practitioners administering the blood thinner could cause a dangerous overdose. The item was dropped.

We also discussed operating room fires, a notorious problem. Surgical teams rely on high-voltage electrical equipment, cautery devices that occasionally arc while in use, and supplies of high-concentration oxygen—all sometimes in close proximity. As a result, most facilities in the world have experienced a surgical fire. These fires are terrifying. Pure oxygen can make almost anything instantly flammable—the surgical drapes over a patient, for instance, and even the airway tube inserted into the throat. But surgical fires are also entirely preventable. If teams ensure there are no oxygen leaks, keep oxygen settings at the lowest acceptable concentration, minimize the use of alcohol-containing antiseptics, and prevent oxygen from flowing onto the surgical field, fires will not occur. A little advance preparation can also avert harm to patients should a fire break out—in particular, verifying that everyone knows the location of the gas valves, alarms, and fire extinguishers. Such steps could easily be included on a checklist.

But compared with the big global killers in surgery, such as infection, bleeding, and unsafe anesthesia, fire is exceedingly rare. Of the tens of millions of operations per year in the United States, it appears only about a hundred involve a surgical fire and vanishingly few of those a fatality. By comparison, some 300,000 operations result in a surgical site infection, and more than eight thousand deaths are associated with these infections. We have done far better at preventing fires than infections. Since the checks required to entirely eliminate fires would make the list substantially longer, these were dropped as well.

There was nothing particularly scientific or even consistent about the decision-making process. Operating on the wrong patient or the wrong side of the body is exceedingly rare too. But the checks to prevent such errors are relatively quick and already accepted in several countries, including the United States. Such mistakes also get a lot of attention. So those checks stayed in.

In contrast, our checks to prevent communication breakdowns tackled a broad and widely recognized source of failure. But our approach—having people formally introduce themselves and briefly discuss critical aspects of a given case—was far from proven effective. Improving teamwork was so fundamental to making a difference, however, that we were willing to leave these measures in and give them a try.

After our London meeting, we did more small-scale testing—just one case at a time. We had a team in London try the draft checklist and give us suggestions, then a team in Hong Kong. With each successive round, the checklist got better. After a certain point, it seemed we had done all we could. We had a checklist we were ready to circulate.

The final WHO safe surgery checklist spelled out nineteen checks in all. Before anesthesia, there are seven checks. The team members confirm that the patient (or the patient's proxy) has personally verified his or her identity and also given consent for the procedure. They make sure that the surgical site is marked and that the pulse oximeter—which monitors oxygen levels—is on the patient and working. They check the patient's medication allergies. They review the risk of airway problems—the most dangerous aspect of general anesthesia—and that appropriate equipment and assistance for them are available. And lastly, if there is a possibility of losing more than half a liter of blood (or the equivalent for a child), they verify that necessary intravenous lines, blood, and fluids are ready.

After anesthesia, but before incision, come seven more checks. The team members make sure they've been introduced by name and role. They confirm that everyone has the correct patient and procedure (including which side of the body—left versus right) in mind. They confirm that antibiotics were either given on time or were unnecessary. They check that any radiology images needed for the operation are displayed. And to make sure everyone is briefed as a team, they discuss the critical aspects of the case: the surgeon reviews how long the operation will take, the amount of blood loss the team should prepare for, and anything else people should be aware of; the anesthesia staff review their anesthetic plans and concerns; and the nursing staff review equipment availability, sterility, and their patient concerns.

Finally, at the end of the operation, before the team wheels the patient from the room, come five final checks. The circulating nurse verbally reviews the recorded name of the completed procedure for accuracy, the labeling of any tissue specimens going to the pathologist, whether all needles, sponges, and instruments have been accounted for, and whether any equipment problems need to be addressed before the next case. Everyone on the team also reviews aloud their plans and concerns for the patient's recovery after surgery, to ensure information is complete and clearly transmitted.

Operations require many more than nineteen steps, of course. But like builders, we tried to encompass the simple to the complex, with several narrowly specified checks to ensure stupid stuff isn't missed (antibiotics, allergies, the wrong patient) and a few communication checks to ensure people work as a team to recognize the many other potential traps and subtleties. At least that was the idea. But would it work and actually make a measurable difference in reducing harm to patients? That was the question.

To find the answer, we decided to study the effect of the safe surgery checklist on patient care in eight hospitals around the world. This number was large enough to provide meaningful results while remaining manageable for my small research team and the modest budget WHO agreed to furnish. We got dozens of applications from hospitals seeking to participate. We set a few criteria for selection. The hospital's leader had to speak English—we could translate the checklist for staff members but we didn't have the resources for daily communication with eight site leaders in multiple languages. The location had to be safe for travel. We received, for instance, an enthusiastic application from the chief of surgery in an Iraqi hospital, which would have been fascinating, but conducting a research trial in a war zone seemed unwise.

I also wanted a wide diversity of participating hospitals—hospitals in rich countries, poor countries, and in between. This insistence caused a degree of consternation at WHO headquarters. As officials explained, WHO's first priority is, quite legitimately, to help the poorer parts of the world, and the substantial costs of paying for data collection in wealthier countries would divert resources from elsewhere. But I had seen surgery in places ranging from rural India to Harvard and seen failure across the span. I thought the checklist might make a difference anywhere. And if it worked in high-income countries, that success might help persuade poorer facilities to take it up. So we agreed to include wealthier sites if they agreed to support most, if not all, the research costs themselves.

Lastly, the hospitals had to be willing to allow observers to measure their actual rates of complications, deaths, and systems failures in surgical care before and after adopting the checklist. Granting this permission was no small matter for hospitals. Most—even those in the highest income settings—have no idea of their current rates. Close observation was bound to embarrass some. Nonetheless, we got eight willing hospitals lined up from all over the globe.

Four were in high-income countries and among the leading hospitals in the world: the University of Washington Medical Center in Seattle, Toronto General Hospital in Canada, St. Mary's Hospital in London, and Auckland City Hospital, New Zealand's largest. Four were intensely busy hospitals in low- or middle-income countries: Philippines General Hospital in Manila, which was twice the size of the wealthier hospitals we enrolled; Prince Hamza Hospital in Amman, Jordan, a new government facility built to accommodate Jordan's bursting refugee population; St. Stephen's Hospital in New Delhi, an urban charity hospital; and St. Francis Designated District Hospital in Ifakara, Tanzania, the lone hospital serving a rural population of nearly one million people.

This was an almost ridiculous range of hospitals to study. Annual health care spending in the high-income countries reached thousands of dollars per person, while in India, the Philippines, and East Africa, it did not rise beyond the double digits. So, for example, the budget of the University of Washington Medical Center—over one billion dollars per year—was more than twice that of the entire country of Tanzania. Surgery therefore differed starkly in our eight hospitals. On one end of the spectrum were those with state-of-the-art capabilities allowing them to do everything from robotic prostatectomies to liver transplants, along with factory loads of planned, low-risk, often day-surgery procedures like hernia repairs, breast biopsies, and ear-tube placements for drainage of chronic ear infections in children. On the other end were hospitals forced by lack of staff and resources to prioritize urgent operations—emergency cesarean sections for mothers dying in childbirth, for example, or procedures for repair of severe traumatic injuries. Even when the hospitals did the same operations—an appendectomy, a mastectomy, the placement of a rod in a broken femur—the conditions were so disparate that the procedures were the same only in name. In the poorer hospitals, the equipment was meager, the teams' training was more limited, and the patients usually arrived sicker—the appendix having ruptured, the breast cancer having grown twice as large, the femur proving not only broken but infected.

Nonetheless, we went ahead with our eight institutions. The goal, after all, was not to compare one hospital with another but to determine where, if anywhere, the checklist could improve care. We hired local research coordinators for the hospitals and trained them to collect accurate information on deaths and complications. We were conservative about what counted. The complications had to be significant—a pneumonia, a heart attack, bleeding requiring a return to the operating room or more than four units of blood, a documented wound infection, or the like. And the occurrence had to actually be witnessed in the hospital, not reported from elsewhere.

We collected data on the surgical care in up to four operating rooms at each facility for about three months before the checklist went into effect. It was a kind of biopsy of the care received by patients across the range of hospitals in the world. And the results were sobering.

Of the close to four thousand adult surgical patients we followed, more than four hundred developed major complications resulting from surgery. Fifty-six of them died. About half the complications involved infections. Another quarter involved technical failures that required a return trip to the operating room to stop bleeding or repair a problem. The overall complication rates ranged from 6 percent to 21 percent. It's important to note that the operating rooms we were studying tended to handle the hospital's more complex procedures. More straightforward operations have lower injury rates. Nonetheless, the pattern confirmed what we'd understood: surgery is risky and dangerous wherever it is done.

We also found, as we suspected we would, signs of substantial opportunity for improvement everywhere. None of the hospitals, for example, had a routine approach to ensure that teams had identified, and prepared for, cases with high blood-loss risk, or conducted any kind of preoperative team briefing about patients. We tracked performance of six specific safety steps: the timely delivery of antibiotics, the use of a working pulse oximeter, the completion of a formal risk assessment for placing an airway tube, the verbal confirmation of the patient's identity and procedure, the appropriate placement of intravenous lines for patients who develop severe bleeding, and finally a complete accounting of sponges at the end of the procedure. These are basics, the surgical equivalent of unlocking the elevator controls before airplane takeoff. Nevertheless, we found gaps everywhere. The very best missed at least one of these minimum steps 6 percent of the time—once in every sixteen patients. And on average, the hospitals missed one of them in a startling two-thirds of patients, whether in rich countries or poor. That is how flawed and inconsistent surgical care routinely is around the world.

Then, starting in spring 2008, the pilot hospitals began implementing our two-minute, nineteen-step surgery checklist. We knew better than to think that just dumping a pile of copies in their operating rooms was going to change anything. The hospital leaders committed to introducing the concept systematically. They made presentations not only to their surgeons but also to their anesthetists, nurses, and other surgical personnel.

We supplied the hospitals with their failure data so the staff could see what they were trying to address. We gave them some PowerPoint slides and a couple of YouTube videos, one demonstrating "How to Use the Safe Surgery Checklist" and one—a bit more entertaining—entitled "How Not to Use the Safe Surgery Checklist," showing how easy it is to screw everything up.

We also asked the hospital leaders to introduce the checklist in just one operating room at first, ideally in procedures the chief surgeon was doing himself, with senior anesthesia and nursing staff taking part. There would surely be bugs to work out. Each hospital would have to adjust the order and wording of the checklist to suit its particular practices and terminology. Several were using translations. A few had already indicated they wanted to add extra checks. For some hospitals, the checklist would also compel systemic changes—for example, stocking more antibiotic supplies in the operating rooms. We needed the first groups using the checklist to have the seniority and patience to make the necessary modifications and not dismiss the whole enterprise.

Using the checklist involved a major cultural change, as well—a shift in authority, responsibility, and expectations about care—and the hospitals needed to recognize that. We gambled that their staff would be far more likely to adopt the checklist if they saw their leadership accepting it from the outset.

My team and I hit the road, fanning out to visit the pilot sites as the checklist effort got under way. I had never seen surgery performed in so many different kinds of settings. The contrasts were even starker than I had anticipated and the range of problems was infinitely wider.

In Tanzania, the hospital was two hundred miles of some-times one-lane dirt roads from Dar es Salaam, and flooding during the rainy season cut off supplies—such as medications and anesthetic gases—often for weeks at a time. There were thousands of surgery patients, but just five surgeons and four anesthesia staff. None of the anesthetists had a medical degree. The patients' families supplied most of the blood for the blood bank, and when that wasn't enough, staff members rolled up their sleeves. They conserved anesthetic supplies by administering mainly spinal anesthesia—injections of numbing medication directly into the spinal canal. They could do operations under spinal that I never conceived of. They saved and resterilized their surgical gloves, using them over and over until holes appeared. They even made their own surgical gauze, the nurses and anesthesia staff sitting around an old wood table at teatime each afternoon cutting bolts of white cotton cloth to size for the next day's cases.

In Delhi, the charity hospital was not as badly off as the Tanzanian site or hospitals I'd been to in rural India. There were more supplies. The staff members were better trained. But the volume of patients they were asked to care for in this city of thirteen million was beyond comprehension. The hospital had seven fully trained anesthetists, for instance, but they had to perform twenty thousand operations a year. To provide a sense of how ludicrous this is, our New Zealand pilot hospital employed ninety-two anesthetists to manage a similar magnitude of surgery. Yet, for all the equipment shortages, power outages, waiting lists, fourteen-hour days, I heard less unhappiness and complaining from the surgical staff in Delhi than in many American hospitals I've been to.

The differences were not just between rich and poor settings, either. Each site was distinctive. St. Mary's Hospital, for example, our London site, was a compound of red brick and white stone buildings more than century and a half old, sprawling over a city block in Paddington. Alexander Fleming discovered penicillin here in 1928. More recently, under its chairman of surgery, Lord Darzi of Denham, the hospital has become an international pioneer in the development of minimally invasive surgery and surgical simulation. St. Mary's is modern, well equipped, and a draw for London's powerful and well-to-do—Prince William and Prince Harry were born here, for example, and Conservative Party leader David Cameron's severely disabled son was cared for here, as well. But it is hardly posh. It remains a government hospital in the National Health Service, serving any Briton without charge or distinction.

Walking through St. Mary's sixteen operating rooms, I found they looked much the same as the ones where I work in Boston—high-tech, up-to-date. But surgical procedures seemed different at every stage. The patients were put to sleep outside the operating theater, instead of inside, and then wheeled in, which meant that the first part of the checklist would have to be changed. The anesthetists and circulating nurses didn't wear masks, which seemed like sacrilege to me, although I had to admit their necessity is unproven for staff who do not work near the patient's incision. Almost every term the surgical teams used was unfamiliar. We all supposedly spoke English, but I was often unsure what they were talking about.

In Jordan, the working environment was also at once recognizable and alien, but in a different way. The operating rooms in Amman had zero frills—this was a still-developing country and the equipment was older and heavily used—but they had most of the things I am used to as a surgeon, and the level of care seemed very good. One of the surgeons I met was Iraqi. He'd trained in Baghdad and practiced there until the chaos following the American invasion in 2003 forced him to flee with his family, abandoning their home, their savings, and his work. Before Saddam Hussein, in the last years of his rule, gutted the Iraqi medical system, Baghdad had provided some of the best medical care in the Middle East. But, the surgeon said, Jordan now seemed positioned to take that role and he felt fortunate to be there. I learned that more than 200,000 foreign patients travel to Jordan for their health care each year, generating as much as one billion dollars in revenues for the country.

What I couldn't work out, though, was how the country's strict gender divide was negotiated in its operating rooms. I remember sitting outside a restaurant the day I arrived, studying the people passing by. Men and women were virtually always separated. Most women covered their hair. I got to know one of the surgery residents, a young man in his late twenties who was my guide for the visit. We even went out to see a movie together. When I learned he had a girlfriend of two years, a graduate student, I asked him how long it was before he got to see her hair.

"I never have," he said.

"C'mon. Never?"

"Never." He'd seen a few strands. He knew she had dark brown hair. But even in the more modern dating relationship of a partly Westernized, highly educated couple, that was it.

In the operating rooms, all the surgeons were men. Most of the nurses were women. The anesthetists split half and half. Given the hierarchies, I wondered whether the kind of teamwork envisioned by the checklist was even possible. The women wore their head scarves in the operating rooms. Most avoided eye contact with men. I slowly learned, however, that not all was what it seemed. The staff didn't hesitate to discard the formalities when necessary. I saw a gallbladder operation in which the surgeon inadvertently contaminated his glove while adjusting the operating lights. He hadn't noticed. But the nurse had.

"You have to change your glove," the nurse told him in Arabic. (Someone translated for me.)

"It's fine," the surgeon said.

"No, it's not," the nurse said. "Don't be stupid." Then she made him change his glove.

For all the differences among the eight hospitals, I was nonetheless surprised by how readily one could feel at home in an operating room, wherever it might be. Once a case was under way, it was still surgery. You still had a human being on the table, with his hopes and his fears and his body opened up to you, trusting you to do right by him. And you still had a group of people striving to work together with enough skill and commitment to warrant that trust.

The introduction of the checklist was rocky at times. We had our share of logistical hiccups. In Manila, for instance, it turned out there was only one nurse for every four operations, because qualified operating nurses kept getting snapped up by American and Canadian hospitals. The medical students who filled in were often too timid to start the checklist, so the anesthesia staff had to be persuaded to take on the task. In Britain, the local staff had difficulties figuring out the changes needed to accommodate their particular anesthesia practices.

There was a learning curve, as well. However straightforward the checklist might appear, if you are used to getting along without one, incorporating it into the routine is not always a smooth process. Sometimes teams forgot to carry out part of the checklist—especially the sign-out, before taking the patient from the room. Other times they found adhering to it just too hard—though not because doing so was complicated. Instead, the difficulty seemed to be social. It felt strange to people just to get their mouths around the words—for a nurse to say, for example, that if the antibiotics hadn't been given, then everyone needed to stop and give them before proceeding. Each person has his or her style in the operating room, especially surgeons. Some are silent, some are moody, some are chatty. Very few knew immediately how to adapt their style to huddling with everyone—even the nursing student—for a systematic run-through of the plans and possible issues.

The introduction of names and roles at the start of an operating day proved a point of particularly divided view. From Delhi to Seattle, the nurses seemed especially grateful for the step, but the surgeons were sometimes annoyed by it. Nonetheless, most complied.

Most but not all. We were thrown out of operating rooms all over the world. "This checklist is a waste of time," we were told. In a couple places, the hospital leaders wanted to call the curmudgeons on the carpet and force them to use it. We discouraged this. Forcing the obstinate few to adopt the checklist might cause a backlash that would sour others on participating. We asked the leaders to present the checklist as simply a tool for people to try in hopes of improving their results. After all, it remained possible that the detractors were right, that the checklist would prove just another well-meaning effort with no significant effect whatsoever.

Pockets of resistance notwithstanding, the safe surgery check-list effort was well under way within a month in each location, with teams regularly using the checklist in every operating room we were studying. We continued monitoring the patient data. I returned home to wait out the results.

I was nervous about the project. We had planned to examine the results for only a short time period, about three months in each pilot site after introduction of the checklist. That way any changes we observed would likely be the consequence of the checklist and not of long-term, ongoing trends in health or medical care. But I worried whether anything could really change in so short a time. The teams were clearly still getting the hang of things. Perhaps we hadn't given them enough time to learn. I also worried about how meager the intervention was when you got right down to it. We'd provided no new equipment, staff, or clinical resources to hospitals. The poor places were still poor, and we had to wonder whether improvement in their results was really possible without changing that. All we'd done was give them a one-page, nineteen-item list and shown them how to use it. We'd worked hard to make it short and simple, but perhaps we'd made it too short and too simple—not detailed enough. Maybe we shouldn't have listened to the aviation gurus.

We began to hear some encouraging stories, however. In London, during a knee replacement by an orthopedic surgeon who was one of our toughest critics, the checklist brought the team to recognize, before incision and the point of no return, that the knee prosthesis on hand was the wrong size for the patient—and that the right size was not available in the hospital. The surgeon became an instant checklist proponent.

In India, we learned, the checklist led the surgery department to recognize a fundamental flaw in its system of care. Usual procedure was to infuse the presurgery antibiotic into patients in the preoperative waiting area before wheeling them in. But the checklist brought the clinicians to realize that frequent delays in the operating schedule meant the antibiotic had usually worn off hours before incision. So the hospital staff shifted their routine in line with the checklist and waited to give the antibiotic until patients were in the operating room.

In Seattle, a friend who had joined the surgical staff at the University of Washington Medical Center told me how easily the checklist had fit into her operating room's routine. But was it helping them catch errors, I asked?

"No question," she said. They'd caught problems with antibiotics, equipment, overlooked medical issues. But more than that, she thought going through the checklist helped the staff respond better when they ran into trouble later—like bleeding or technical difficulties during the operation. "We just work better together as a team," she said.

The stories gave me hope.

In October 2008, the results came in. I had two research fellows, both of them residents in general surgery, working on the project with me. Alex Haynes had taken more than a year away from surgical training to run the eight-city pilot study and compile the data. Tom Weiser had spent two years managing development of the WHO checklist program, and he'd been in charge of double-checking the numbers. A retired cardiac surgeon, William Berry, was the triple check on everything they did. Late one afternoon, they all came in to see me.

"You've got to see this," Alex said.

He laid a sheaf of statistical printouts in front of me and walked me through the tables. The final results showed that the rate of major complications for surgical patients in all eight hospitals fell by 36 percent after introduction of the checklist. Deaths fell 47 percent. The results had far outstripped what we'd dared to hope for, and all were statistically highly significant. Infections fell by almost half. The number of patients having to return to the operating room after their original operations because of bleeding or other technical problems fell by one-fourth. Overall, in this group of nearly 4,000 patients, 435 would have been expected to develop serious complications based on our earlier observation data. But instead just 277 did. Using the checklist had spared more than 150 people from harm—and 27 of them from death.

You might think that I'd have danced a jig on my desk, that I'd have gone running through the operating room hallways yelling, "It worked! It worked!" But this is not what I did. Instead, I became very, very nervous. I started poking through the pile of data looking for mistakes, for problems, for anything that might upend the results.

Suppose, I said, this improvement wasn't due to the checklist. Maybe, just by happenstance, the teams had done fewer emergency cases and other risky operations in the second half of the study, and that's why their results looked better. Alex went back and ran the numbers again. Nope, it turned out. The teams had actually done slightly more emergency cases in the checklist period than before. And the mix of types of operations— obstetric, thoracic, orthopedic, abdominal—was unchanged.

Suppose this was just a Hawthorne effect, that is to say, a byproduct of being observed in a study rather than proof of the checklist's power. In about 20 percent of the operations, after all, a researcher had been physically present in the operating room collecting information. Maybe the observer's presence was what had improved care. The research team pointed out, however, that the observers had been in the operating rooms from the very beginning of the project, and the results had not leaped upward until the checklist was introduced. Moreover, we'd tracked which operations had an observer and which ones hadn't. And when Alex rechecked the data, the results proved no different—the improvements were equally dramatic for observed and unob-served operations.

Okay, maybe the checklist made a difference in *some* places, but perhaps only in the poor sites. No, that didn't turn out to be the case either. The baseline rate of surgical complications was indeed lower in the four hospitals in high-income countries, but introducing the checklist had produced a one-third decrease in major complications for the patients in those hospitals, as well— also a highly significant reduction.

The team took me through the results for each of the eight hospitals, one by one. In every site, introduction of the checklist had been accompanied by a substantial reduction in complica-tions. In seven out of eight, it was a double-digit percentage drop.

This thing was real.

In January 2009, the *New England Journal of Medicine* published our study as a rapid-release article. Even before then, word began to leak out as we distributed the findings to our pilot sites. Hospitals in Washington State learned of Seattle's results and began trying the checklist themselves. Pretty soon they'd formed a coalition with the state's insurers, Boeing, and the governor to systematically introduce the checklist across the state and track detailed data. In Great Britain, Lord Darzi, the chairman of surgery at St. Mary's Hospital, had meanwhile been made a minister of health. When he and the country's top designate to WHO, Sir Liam Donaldson (who had also pushed for the surgery project in the first place), saw the study results, they launched a campaign to implement the checklist nationwide.

The reaction of surgeons was more mixed. Even if using the checklist didn't take the time many feared—indeed, in several hospitals teams reported that it saved them time—some objected that the study had not clearly established *how* the checklist was producing such dramatic results. This was true. In our eight hospitals, we saw improvements in administering antibiotics to reduce infections, in use of oxygen monitoring during operations, in making sure teams had the right patient and right procedure before making an incision. But these particular improvements could not explain why unrelated complications like bleeding fell, for example. We surmised that improved communication was the key. Spot surveys of random staff members coming out of surgery after the checklist was in effect did indeed report a significant increase in the level of communication. There was also a notable correlation between teamwork scores and results for patients—

the greater the improvement in teamwork, the greater the drop in complications.

Perhaps the most revealing information, however, was simply what the staff told us. More than 250 staff members—surgeons, anesthesiologists, nurses, and others—filled out an anonymous survey after three months of using the checklist. In the beginning, most had been skeptical. But by the end, 80 percent reported that the checklist was easy to use, did not take a long time to complete, and had improved the safety of care. And 78 percent actually observed the checklist to have prevented an error in the operating room.

Nonetheless, some skepticism persisted. After all, 20 percent did not find it easy to use, thought it took too long, and felt it had not improved the safety of care.

Then we asked the staff one more question. "If you were having an operation," we asked, "would you want the checklist to be used?"

A full 93 percent said yes.

8. THE HERO IN THE AGE OF CHECKLISTS

We have an opportunity before us, not just in medicine but in virtually any endeavor. Even the most expert among us can gain from searching out the patterns of mistakes and failures and putting a few checks in place. But will we do it? Are we ready to grab onto the idea? It is far from clear.

Take the safe surgery checklist. If someone discovered a new drug that could cut down surgical complications with anything remotely like the effectiveness of the checklist, we would have television ads with minor celebrities extolling its virtues. Detail men would offer free lunches to get doctors to make it part of their practice. Government programs would research it. Competitors would jump in to make newer and better versions. If the checklist were a medical device, we would have surgeons clamoring for it, lining up at display booths at surgical conferences to give it a try, hounding their hospital administrators to get one for them—because, damn it, doesn't providing good care matter to those pencil pushers?

That's what happened when surgical robots came out—drool-inducing twenty-second-century $1.7 million remote-controlled machines designed to help surgeons do laparoscopic surgery with more maneuverability inside patients' bodies and fewer complications. The robots increased surgical costs massively and have so far improved results only modestly for a few operations, compared with standard laparoscopy. Nonetheless, hospitals in the United States and abroad have spent billions of dollars on them.

But meanwhile, the checklist? Well, it hasn't been ignored. Since the results of the WHO safe surgery checklist were made public, more than a dozen countries—including Australia, Brazil, Canada, Costa Rica, Ecuador, France, Ireland, Jordan, New Zealand, the Philippines, Spain, and the United Kingdom—have publicly committed to implementing versions of it in hospitals nationwide. Some are taking the additional step of tracking results, which is crucial for ensuring the checklist is being put in place successfully. In the United States, hospital associations in twenty states have pledged to do the same. By the end of 2009, about 10 percent of American hospitals had either adopted the checklist or taken steps to implement it, and worldwide more than two thousand hospitals had.

This is all encouraging. Nonetheless, we doctors remain a long way from actually embracing the idea. The checklist has arrived in our operating rooms mostly from the outside in and from the top down. It has come from finger-wagging health officials, who are regarded by surgeons as more or less the enemy, or from jug-eared hospital safety officers, who are about as beloved as the playground safety patrol. Sometimes it is the chief of surgery who brings it in, which means we complain under our breath rather than raise a holy tirade. But it is regarded as an irritation, as interference on our terrain. This is my patient. This is my operating room. And the way I carry out an operation is my business and my responsibility. So who do these people think they are, telling me what to do?

Now, if surgeons end up using the checklist anyway, what is the big deal if we do so without joy in our souls? We're doing it. That's what matters, right?

Not necessarily. Just ticking boxes is not the ultimate goal here. Embracing a culture of teamwork and discipline is. And if we recognize the opportunity, the two-minute WHO checklist is just a start. It is a single, broad-brush device intended to catch a few problems common to all operations, and we surgeons could build on it to do even more. We could adopt, for example, specialized checklists for hip replacement procedures, pancreatic operations, aortic aneurysm repairs, examining each of our major procedures for their most common avoidable glitches and incorporating checks to help us steer clear of them. We could even devise emergency checklists, like aviation has, for nonroutine situations—such as the cardiac arrest my friend John described in which the doctors forgot that an overdose of potassium could be a cause.

Beyond the operating room, moreover, there are hundreds, perhaps thousands, of things doctors do that are as dangerous and prone to error as surgery. Take, for instance, the treatment of heart attacks, strokes, drug overdoses, pneumonias, kidney failures, seizures. And consider the many other situations that are only seemingly simpler and less dire—the evaluation of a patient with a headache, for example, a funny chest pain, a lung nodule, a breast lump. All involve risk, uncertainty, and complexity—and therefore steps that are worth committing to a checklist and testing in routine care. Good checklists could become as important for doctors and nurses as good stethoscopes (which, unlike checklists, have never been proved to make a difference in patient care). The hard question—still unanswered—is whether medical culture can seize the opportunity.

Tom Wolfe's *The Right Stuff* tells the story of our first astronauts and charts the demise of the maverick, Chuck Yeager test-pilot culture of the 1950s. It was a culture defined by how unbelievably dangerous the job was. Test pilots strapped themselves into machines of barely controlled power and complexity, and a quarter of them were killed on the job. The pilots had to have focus, daring, wits, and an ability to improvise—the right stuff. But as knowledge of how to control the risks of flying accumulated—as checklists and flight simulators became more prevalent and sophisticated—the danger diminished, values of safety and conscientiousness prevailed, and the rock star status of the test pilots was gone.

Something like this is going on in medicine. We have the means to make some of the most complex and dangerous work we do—in surgery, emergency care, ICU medicine, and beyond—more effective than we ever thought possible. But the prospect pushes against the traditional culture of medicine, with its central belief that in situations of high risk and complexity what you want is a kind of expert audacity—the right stuff, again. Checklists and standard operating procedures feel like exactly the opposite, and that's what rankles many people.

It's ludicrous, though, to suppose that checklists are going to do away with the need for courage, wits, and improvisation. The work of medicine is too intricate and individual for that: good clinicians will not be able to dispense with expert audacity. Yet we should also be ready to accept the virtues of regimentation.

And it is true well beyond medicine. The opportunity is evident in many fields—and so also is the resistance. Finance offers one example. Recently, I spoke to Mohnish Pabrai, managing partner in Pabrai Investment Funds in Irvine, California. He is one of three investors I've recently met who have taken a page from medicine and aviation to incorporate formal checklists into their work. All three are huge investors: Pabrai runs a $500 million portfolio; Guy Spier is head of Aquamarine Capital Management in Zurich, Switzerland, a $70 million fund. The third did not want to be identified by name or to reveal the size of the fund where he is a director, but it is one of the biggest in the world and worth billions. The three consider themselves "value investors"—investors who buy shares in underrecognized, undervalued companies. They don't time the market. They don't buy according to some computer algorithm. They do intensive research, look for good deals, and invest for the long run. They aim to buy Coca-Cola before everyone realizes it's going to be Coca-Cola.

Pabrai described what this involves. Over the last fifteen years, he's made a new investment or two per quarter, and he's found it requires in-depth investigation of ten or more prospects for each one he finally buys stock in. The ideas can bubble up from anywhere—a billboard advertisement, a newspaper article about real estate in Brazil, a mining journal he decides to pick up for some random reason. He reads broadly and looks widely. He has his eyes open for the glint of a diamond in the dirt, of a business about to boom.

He hits upon hundreds of possibilities but most drop away after cursory examination. Every week or so, though, he spots one that starts his pulse racing. It seems surefire. He can't believe no one else has caught onto it yet. He begins to think it could make him tens of millions of dollars if he plays it right, no, this time maybe hundreds of millions.

"You go into greed mode," he said. Guy Spier called it "cocaine brain." Neuroscientists have found that the prospect of making money stimulates the same primitive reward circuits in the brain that cocaine does. And that, Pabrai said, is when serious investors like himself try to become systematic. They focus on dispassionate analysis, on avoiding both irrational exuberance and panic. They pore over the company's financial reports, investigate its liabilities and risks, examine its management team's track record, weigh its competitors, consider the future of the market it is in— trying to gauge both the magnitude of opportunity and the margin of safety.

The patron saint of value investors is Warren Buffett, among the most successful financiers in history and one of the two richest men in the world, even after the losses he suffered in the crash of 2008. Pabrai has studied every deal Buffett and his company, Berkshire Hathaway, have made—good or bad—and read every book he could find about them. He even pledged $650,000 at a charity auction to have lunch with Buffett.

"Warren," Pabrai said—and after a $650,000 lunch, I guess first names are in order—"Warren uses a 'mental checklist' process" when looking at potential investments. So that's more or less what Pabrai did from his fund's inception. He was disciplined. He made sure to take his time when studying a company. The process could require weeks. And he did very well following this method—but not always, he found. He also made mistakes, some of them disastrous.

These were not mistakes merely in the sense that he lost money on his bets or missed making money on investments he'd rejected. That's bound to happen. Risk is unavoidable in Pabrai's line of work. No, these were mistakes in the sense that he had miscalculated the risks involved, made errors of analysis. For example, looking back, he noticed that he had repeatedly erred in determining how "leveraged" companies were—how much cash was really theirs, how much was borrowed, and how risky those debts were. The information was available; he just hadn't looked for it carefully enough.

In large part, he believes, the mistakes happened because he wasn't able to damp down the cocaine brain. Pabrai is a forty-five-year-old former engineer. He comes from India, where he clawed his way up its fiercely competitive educational system. Then he secured admission to Clemson University, in South Carolina, to study engineering. From there he climbed the ranks of technology companies in Chicago and California. Before going into investment, he built a successful informational technology company of his own. All this is to say he knows a thing or two about being dispassionate and avoiding the lure of instant gratification. Yet no matter how objective he tried to be about a potentially exciting investment, he said, he found his brain working against him, latching onto evidence that confirmed his initial hunch and dismissing the signs of a downside. It's what the brain does.

"You get seduced," he said. "You start cutting corners."

Or, in the midst of a bear market, the opposite happens. You go into "fear mode," he said. You see people around you losing their bespoke shirts, and you overestimate the dangers.

He also found he made mistakes in handling complexity. A good decision requires looking at so many different features of companies in so many ways that, even without the cocaine brain, he was missing obvious patterns. His mental checklist wasn't good enough. "I am not Warren," he said. "I don't have a 300 IQ." He needed an approach that could work for someone with an ordinary IQ. So he devised a written checklist.

Apparently, Buffett himself could have used one. Pabrai noticed that even he made certain repeated mistakes. "That's when I knew he wasn't really using a checklist," Pabrai said.

So Pabrai made a list of mistakes he'd seen—ones Buffett and other investors had made as well as his own. It soon contained dozens of different mistakes, he said. Then, to help him guard against them, he devised a matching list of checks—about seventy in all. One, for example, came from a Berkshire Hathaway mistake he'd studied involving the company's purchase in early 2000 of Cort Furniture, a Virginia-based rental furniture business. Over the previous ten years, Cort's business and profits had climbed impressively. Charles Munger, Buffett's longtime investment partner, believed Cort was riding a fundamental shift in the American economy. The business environment had become more and more volatile and companies therefore needed to grow and shrink more rapidly than ever before. As a result, they were increasingly apt to lease office space rather than buy it—and, Munger noticed, to lease the furniture, too. Cort was in a perfect position to benefit. Everything else about the company was measuring up—it had solid financials, great management, and so on. So Munger bought. But buying was an error. He had missed the fact that the three previous years of earnings had been driven entirely by the dot-com boom of the late nineties. Cort was leasing furniture to hundreds of start-up companies that suddenly stopped paying their bills and evaporated when the boom collapsed.

"Munger and Buffett saw the dot-com bubble a mile away," Pabrai said. "These guys were completely clear." But they missed how dependent Cort was on it. Munger later called his purchase "a macroeconomic mistake."

"Cort's earning power basically went from substantial to zero for a while," he confessed to his shareholders.

So Pabrai added the following checkpoint to his list: when analyzing a company, stop and confirm that you've asked yourself whether the revenues might be overstated or understated due to boom or bust conditions.

Like him, the anonymous investor I spoke to—I'll call him Cook—made a checklist. But he was even more methodical: he enumerated the errors known to occur at any point in the investment process—during the research phase, during decision making, during execution of the decision, and even in the period after making an investment when one should be monitoring for problems. He then designed detailed checklists to avoid the errors, complete with clearly identified pause points at which he and his investment team would run through the items.

He has a Day Three Checklist, for example, which he and his team review at the end of the third day of considering an investment. By that point, the checklist says, they should confirm that they have gone over the prospect's key financial statements for the previous ten years, including checking for specific items in each statement and possible patterns across the statements.

"It's easy to hide in a statement. It's hard to hide between statements," Cook said.

One check, for example, requires the members of the team to verify that they've read the footnotes on the cash flow statements. Another has them confirm they've reviewed the statement of key management risks. A third asks them to make sure they've looked to see whether cash flow and costs match the reported revenue growth.

"This is basic basic basic," he said. "Just look! You'd be amazed by how often people don't do it." Consider the Enron debacle, he said. "People could have figured out it was a disaster entirely from the financial statements."

He told me about one investment he looked at that seemed a huge winner. The cocaine brain was screaming. It turned out, however, that the company's senior officers, who'd been selling prospective investors on how great their business was, had quietly sold every share they owned. The company was about to tank and buyers jumping aboard had no idea. But Cook had put a check on his three-day list that ensured his team had reviewed the fine print of the company's mandatory stock disclosures, and he discovered the secret. Forty-nine times out of fifty, he said, there's nothing to be found. "But then there is."

The checklist doesn't tell him what to do, he explained. It is not a formula. But the checklist helps him be as smart as possible every step of the way, ensuring that he's got the critical information he needs when he needs it, that he's systematic about decision making, that he's talked to everyone he should. With a good checklist in hand, he was convinced he and his partners could make decisions as well as human beings are able. And as a result, he was also convinced they could reliably beat the market.

I asked him whether he wasn't fooling himself.

"Maybe," he said. But he put it in surgical terms for me. "When surgeons make sure to wash their hands or to talk to everyone on the team"—he'd seen the surgery checklist—"they improve their outcomes with no increase in skill. That's what we are doing when we use the checklist."

Cook would not discuss precise results—his fund does not disclose its earnings publicly—but he said he had already seen the checklist deliver better outcomes for him. He had put the check-list process in place at the start of 2008 and, at a minimum, it appeared that he had been able to ride out the subsequent eco-nomic collapse without disaster. Others say his fund has done far better than that, outperforming its peers. How much of any suc-cess can be directly credited to the checklist is not clear—after all, he's used it just two years so far. What Cook says is certain, how-ever, was that in a period of enormous volatility the checklist gave his team at least one additional and unexpected edge over others: efficiency.

When he first introduced the checklist, he assumed it would slow his team down, increasing the time and work required for their investment decisions. He was prepared to pay that price. The benefits of making fewer mistakes seemed obvious. And in fact, using the checklist did increase the up-front work time. But to his surprise, he found they were able to evaluate many more investments in far less time overall.

Before the checklist, Cook said, it sometimes took weeks and multiple meetings to sort out how seriously they should consider a candidate investment—whether they should drop it or pursue a more in-depth investigation. The process was open-ended and haphazard, and when people put a month into researching an investment, they tended to get, well, invested. After the checklist, though, he and his team found that they could consistently sort out by the three-day check which prospects really deserved further consideration and which ones didn't. "The process was more thorough but faster," he said. "It was one hit, and we could move on."

Pabrai and Spier, the Zurich investor, found the same phenomenon. Spier used to employ an investment analyst. But "I didn't need him anymore," he said. Pabrai had been working with a checklist for about a year. His fund was up more than 100 percent since then. This could not possibly be attributed to just the checklist. With the checklist in place, however, he observed that he could move through investment decisions far faster and more methodically. As the markets plunged through late 2008 and stockholders dumped shares in panic, there were numerous deals to be had. And in a single quarter he was able to investigate more than a hundred companies and add ten to his fund's portfolios. Without the checklist, Pabrai said, he could not have gotten through a fraction of the analytic work or have had the confidence to rely on it. A year later, his investments were up more than 160 percent on average. He'd made no mistakes at all.

What makes these investors' experiences striking to me is not merely their evidence that checklists might work as well in finance as they do in medicine. It's that here, too, they have found takers slow to come. In the money business, everyone looks for an edge. If someone is doing well, people pounce like starved hyenas to find out how. Almost every idea for making even slightly more money—investing in Internet companies, buying tranches of sliced-up mortgages, whatever—gets sucked up by the giant maw almost instantly. Every idea, that is, except one: checklists.

I asked Cook how much interest others have had in what he has been doing these past two years. Zero, he said—or actually that's not quite true. People have been intensely interested in what he's been buying and how, but the minute the word *checklist* comes out of his mouth, they disappear. Even in his own firm, he's found it a hard sell.

"I got pushback from everyone. It took my guys months to finally see the value," he said. To this day, his partners still don't all go along with his approach and don't use the checklist in their decisions when he's not involved.

"I find it amazing other investors have not even bothered to try," he said. "Some have asked. None have done it."

The resistance is perhaps an inevitable response. Some years ago, Geoff Smart, a Ph.D. psychologist who was then at Claremont Graduate University, conducted a revealing research project. He studied fifty-one venture capitalists, people who make gutsy, high-risk, multimillion-dollar investments in unproven start-up companies. Their work is quite unlike that of money managers like Pabrai and Cook and Spier, who invest in established companies with track records and public financial statements one can analyze. Venture capitalists bet on wild-eyed, greasy-haired, underaged entrepreneurs pitching ideas that might be little more than scribbles on a sheet of paper or a clunky prototype that barely works. But that's how Google and Apple started out, and the desperate belief of venture capitalists is that they can find the next equivalent and own it.

Smart specifically studied how such people made their most difficult decision in judging whether to give an entrepreneur money or not. You would think that this would be whether the entrepreneur's idea is actually a good one. But finding a good idea is apparently not all that hard. Finding an entrepreneur who can execute a good idea is a different matter entirely. One needs a person who can take an idea from proposal to reality, work the long hours, build a team, handle the pressures and setbacks, manage technical and people problems alike, and stick with the effort for years on end without getting distracted or going insane. Such people are rare and extremely hard to spot.

Smart identified half a dozen different ways the venture capitalists he studied decided whether they'd found such a person. These were styles of thinking, really. He called one type of investor the "Art Critics." They assessed entrepreneurs almost at a glance, the way an art critic can assess the quality of a painting—intuitively and based on long experience. "Sponges" took more time gathering information about their targets, soaking up whatever they could from interviews, on-site visits, references, and the like. Then they went with whatever their guts told them. As one such investor told Smart, he did "due diligence by mucking around."

The "Prosecutors" interrogated entrepreneurs aggressively, testing them with challenging questions about their knowledge and how they would handle random hypothetical situations. "Suitors" focused more on wooing people than on evaluating them. "Terminators" saw the whole effort as doomed to failure and skipped the evaluation part. They simply bought what they thought were the best ideas, fired entrepreneurs they found to be incompetent, and hired replacements.

Then there were the investors Smart called the "Airline Captains." They took a methodical, checklist-driven approach to their task. Studying past mistakes and lessons from others in the field, they built formal checks into their process. They forced themselves to be disciplined and not to skip steps, even when they found someone they "knew" intuitively was a real prospect.

Smart next tracked the venture capitalists' success over time. There was no question which style was most effective—and by now you should be able to guess which one. It was the Airline Captain, hands down. Those taking the checklist-driven approach had a 10 percent likelihood of later having to fire senior management for incompetence or concluding that their original evaluation was inaccurate. The others had at least a 50 percent likelihood.

The results showed up in their bottom lines, too. The Airline Captains had a median 80 percent return on the investments studied, the others 35 percent or less. Those with other styles were not failures by any stretch—experience does count for something. But those who added checklists to their experience proved substantially more successful.

The most interesting discovery was that, despite the disadvantages, most investors were either Art Critics or·Sponges—intuitive decision makers instead of systematic analysts. Only one in eight took the Airline Captain approach. Now, maybe the others didn't know about the Airline Captain approach. But even knowing seems to make little difference. Smart published his findings more than a decade ago. He has since gone on to explain them in a best-selling business book on hiring called *Who*. But when I asked him, now that the knowledge is out, whether the proportion of major investors taking the more orderly, checklist-driven approach has increased substantially, he could only report, "No. It's the same."

We don't like checklists. They can be painstaking. They're not much fun. But I don't think the issue here is mere laziness. There's something deeper, more visceral going on when people walk away not only from saving lives but from making money. It somehow feels beneath us to use a checklist, an embarrassment. It runs counter to deeply held beliefs about how the truly great among us—those we aspire to be—handle situations of high stakes and complexity. The truly great are daring. They improvise. They do not have protocols and checklists.

Maybe our idea of heroism needs updating.

On January 14, 2009, WHO's safe surgery checklist was made public. As it happened, the very next day, US Airways Flight 1549 took off from La Guardia Airport in New York City with 155 people on board, struck a large flock of Canada geese over Manhattan, lost both engines, and famously crash-landed in the icy Hudson River. The fact that not a single life was lost led the press to christen the incident the "miracle on the Hudson." A National Transportation Safety Board official said the flight "has to go down as the most successful ditching in aviation history." Fifty-seven-year-old Captain Chesley B. "Sully" Sullenberger III, a former air force pilot with twenty thousand hours of flight experience, was hailed the world over.

"Quiet Air Hero Is Captain America," shouted the *New York Post* headline. ABC News called him the "Hudson River hero." The German papers hailed "Der Held von New York," the French "Le Nouveau Héros de l'Amérique," the Spanish-language press "El Héroe de Nueva York." President George W. Bush phoned Sullenberger to thank him personally, and President-elect Barack

Obama invited him and his family to attend his inauguration five days later. Photographers tore up the lawn of his Danville, California, home trying to get a glimpse of his wife and teenage children. He was greeted with a hometown parade and a $3 million book deal.

But as the details trickled out about the procedures and checklists that were involved, the fly-by-wire computer system that helped control the glide down to the water, the copilot who shared flight responsibilities, the cabin crew who handled the remarkably swift evacuation, we the public started to become uncertain about exactly who the hero here was. As Sullenberger kept saying over and over from the first of his interviews afterward, "I want to correct the record right now. This was a crew effort." The outcome, he said, was the result of teamwork and adherence to procedure as much as of any individual skill he may have had.

Aw, that's just the modesty of the quiet hero, we finally insisted. The next month, when the whole crew of five—not just Sullenberger—was brought out to receive the keys to New York City, for "exclusive" interviews on every network, and for a standing ovation by an audience of seventy thousand at the Super Bowl in Tampa Bay, you could see the press had already determined how to play this. They didn't want to talk about teamwork and procedure. They wanted to talk about Sully using his experience flying gliders as an Air Force Academy cadet.

"That was so long ago," Sullenberger said, "and those gliders are so different from a modern jet airliner. I think the transfer of experience was not large."

It was as if we simply could not process the full reality of what had been required to save the people on that plane.

The aircraft was a European-built Airbus A320 with two jet engines, one on each wing. The plane took off at 3:25 p.m. on a cold but clear afternoon, headed for Charlotte, North Carolina, with First Officer Jeffrey Skiles at the controls and Sullenberger serving as the pilot not flying. The first thing to note is that the two had never flown together before that trip. Both were tremendously experienced. Skiles had nearly as many flight hours as Sullenberger and had been a longtime Boeing 737 captain until downsizing had forced him into the right-hand seat and retraining to fly A320s. This much experience may sound like a good thing, but it isn't necessarily. Imagine two experienced but unacquainted lawyers meeting to handle your case on your opening day in court. Or imagine two top basketball coaches who are complete strangers stepping onto the parquet to lead a team in a championship game. Things could go fine, but it is more likely that they will go badly.

Before the pilots started the plane's engines at the gate, however, they adhered to a strict discipline—the kind most other professions avoid. They ran through their checklists. They made sure they'd introduced themselves to each other and the cabin crew. They did a short briefing, discussing the plan for the flight, potential concerns, and how they'd handle troubles if they ran into them. And by adhering to this discipline—by taking just those few short minutes—they not only made sure the plane was fit to travel but also transformed themselves from individuals into a team, one systematically prepared to handle whatever came their way.

I don't think we recognize how easy it would have been for Sullenberger and Skiles to have blown off those preparations, to have cut corners that day. The crew had more than 150 total years of flight experience—150 years of running their checklists over and over and over, practicing them in simulators, studying the annual updates. The routine can seem pointless most of the time. Not once had any of them been in an airplane accident. They fully expected to complete their careers without experiencing one, either. They considered the odds of anything going wrong extremely low, far lower than we do in medicine or investment or legal practice or other fields. But they ran through their checks anyway.

It need not have been this way. As recently as the 1970s, some airline pilots remained notoriously bluff about their preparations, however carefully designed. "I've never had a problem," they would say. Or "Let's get going. Everything's fine." Or "I'm the captain. This is my ship. And you're wasting my time." Consider, for example, the infamous 1977 Tenerife disaster. It was the deadliest accident in aviation history. Two Boeing 747 airliners collided at high speed in fog on a Canary Islands runway, killing 583 people on board. The captain on one of the planes, a KLM flight, had misunderstood air traffic control instructions conveying that he was *not* cleared for takeoff on the runway—and disregarded the second officer, who recognized that the instructions were unclear. There was in fact a Pan American flight still taxiing on the same runway.

"Is he not cleared, that Pan American?" the second officer said to the captain.

"Oh yes," the captain insisted, and continued onto the runway.

The captain was wrong. The second officer sensed it. But they were not prepared for this moment. They had not taken the steps to make themselves a team. As a result, the second officer never believed he had the permission, let alone the duty, to halt the captain and clear up the confusion. Instead the captain was allowed to plow ahead and kill them all.

The fear people have about the idea of adherence to protocol is rigidity. They imagine mindless automatons, heads down in a checklist, incapable of looking out their windshield and coping with the real world in front of them. But what you find, when a checklist is well made, is exactly the opposite. The checklist gets the dumb stuff out of the way, the routines your brain shouldn't have to occupy itself with (Are the elevator controls set? Did the patient get her antibiotics on time? Did the managers sell all their shares? Is everyone on the same page here?), and lets it rise above to focus on the hard stuff (Where should we land?).

Here are the details of one of the sharpest checklists I've seen, a checklist for engine failure during flight in a single-engine Cessna airplane—the US Airways situation, only with a solo pilot. It is slimmed down to six key steps not to miss for restarting the engine, steps like making sure the fuel shutoff valve is in the OPEN position and putting the backup fuel pump switch ON. But step one on the list is the most fascinating. It is simply: FLY THE AIRPLANE. Because pilots sometimes become so desperate trying to restart their engine, so crushed by the cognitive overload of thinking through what could have gone wrong, they forget this most basic task. FLY THE AIRPLANE. This isn't rigidity. This is making sure everyone has their best shot at survival.

About ninety seconds after takeoff, US Airways Flight 1549 was climbing up through three thousand feet when it crossed the path of the geese. The plane came upon the geese so suddenly Sullenberger's immediate reaction was to duck. The sound of the birds hitting the windshield and the engines was loud enough to be heard on the cockpit voice recorder. As news reports later pointed out, planes have hit hundreds of thousands of birds without incident. But dual bird strikes are rare. And, in any case, jet engines are made to handle most birds, more or less liquefying them. Canada geese, however, are larger than most birds, often ten pounds and up, and no engine can handle them. Jet engines are designed instead to shut down after ingesting one, without exploding or sending metal shrapnel into the wings or the passengers on board. That's precisely what the A320's engines did when they were hit with the rarest of rare situations—at least three geese in the two engines. They immediately lost power.

Once that happened, Sullenberger made two key decisions: first, to take over flying the airplane from his copilot, Skiles, and, second, to land in the Hudson. Both seemed clear choices at the time and were made almost instinctively. Within a minute it became apparent that the plane had too little speed to make it to La Guardia or to the runway in Teterboro, New Jersey, offered by air traffic control. As for taking over the piloting, both he and Skiles had decades of flight experience, but Sullenberger had logged far more hours flying the A320. All the key landmarks to avoid hitting—Manhattan's skyscrapers, the George Washington Bridge—were out his left-side window. And Skiles had also just completed A320 emergency training and was more recently familiar with the checklists they would need.

"My aircraft," Sullenberger said, using the standard language as he put his hands on the controls.

"Your aircraft," Skiles replied. There was no argument about what to do next, not even a discussion. And there was no need for one. The pilots' preparations had made them a team. Sullenberger would look for the nearest, safest possible landing site. Skiles would go to the engine failure checklists and see if he could relight the engines. But for the computerized voice of the ground proximity warning system saying "Pull up. Pull up. Pull up. Pull up," the cockpit was virtually silent as each pilot concentrated on his tasks and observed the other for cues that kept them coordinated.

Both men played crucial roles here. We treat copilots as if they are superfluous—backups who are given a few tasks so that they have something to do. But given the complexity of modern airplanes, they are as integral to a successful flight as anesthesiologists are to a successful operation. Pilot and copilot alternate taking the flight controls and managing the flight equipment and checklist responsibilities, and when things go wrong it's not at all clear which is the harder job. The plane had only three and a half minutes of glide in it. In that time, Skiles needed to make sure he'd done everything possible to relight the engines while also preparing the aircraft for ditching if it wasn't feasible. But the steps required just to restart one engine typically take more time than that. He had some choices to make.

Plunging out of the sky, he judged that their best chance at survival would come from getting an engine restarted. So he decided to focus almost entirely on the engine failure checklist and running through it as fast as he could. The extent of damage to the engines was unknown, but regaining even partial power would have been sufficient to get the plane to an airport. In the end, Skiles managed to complete a restart attempt on both engines, something investigators later testified to be "very remarkable" in the time frame he had—and something they found difficult to replicate in simulation.

Yet he did not ignore the ditching procedure, either. He did not have time to do everything on the checklist. But he got the distress signals sent, and he made sure the plane was properly configured for an emergency water landing.

"Flaps out?" asked Sullenberger.

"Got flaps out," responded Skiles.

Sullenberger focused on the glide down to the water. But even in this, he was not on his own. For, as journalist and pilot William Langewiesche noted afterward, the plane's fly-by-wire control system was designed to assist pilots in accomplishing a perfect glide without demanding unusual skills. It eliminated drift and wobble. It automatically coordinated the rudder with the roll of the wings. It gave Sullenberger a green dot on his screen to target for optimal descent. And it maintained the ideal angle to achieve lift, while preventing the plane from accidentally reaching "radical angles" during flight that would have caused it to lose its gliding ability. The system freed him to focus on other critical tasks, like finding a landing site near ferries in order to give passengers their best chance of rescue and keeping the wings level as the plane hit the water's surface.

Meanwhile, the three flight attendants in the cabin—Sheila Dail, Donna Dent, and Doreen Welsh—followed through on their protocols for such situations. They had the passengers put their heads down and grab their legs to brace for impact. Upon landing and seeing water through the windows, the flight attendants gave instructions to don life vests. They made sure the doors got open swiftly when the plane came to a halt, that passengers didn't waste time grabbing for their belongings, or trap themselves by inflating life vests inside the aircraft. Welsh, stationed in the very back, had to wade through ice cold, chest-high water leaking in through the torn fuselage to do her part. Just two of the four exits were safely accessible. Nonetheless, working together they got everyone out of a potentially sinking plane in just three minutes—exactly as designed.

While the evacuation got under way, Sullenberger headed back to check on the passengers and the condition of the plane. Meanwhile, Skiles remained up in the cockpit to run the evacuation checklist—making sure potential fire hazards were dealt with, for instance. Only when it was completed did he emerge. The arriving flotilla of ferries and boats proved more than sufficient to get everyone out of the water. Air in the fuel tanks, which were only partly full, kept the plane stable and afloat. Sullenberger had time for one last check of the plane. He walked the aisle to make sure no one had been forgotten, and then he exited himself.

The entire event had gone shockingly smoothly. After the plane landed, Sullenberger said, "First Officer Jeff Skiles and I turned to each other and, almost in unison, at the same time, with the same words, said to each other, 'Well, that wasn't as bad as I thought.' "

So who was the hero here? No question, there was something miraculous about this flight. Luck played a huge role. The incident occurred in daylight, allowing the pilots to spot a safe landing site. Plenty of boats were nearby for quick rescue before hypothermia set in. The bird strike was sufficiently high to let the plane clear the George Washington Bridge. The plane was also headed downstream, with the current, instead of upstream or over the ocean, limiting damage on landing.

Nonetheless, even with fortune on their side, there remained every possibility that 155 lives could have been lost that day. But what rescued them was something more exceptional, difficult, crucial, and, yes, heroic than flight ability. The crew of US Airways Flight 1549 showed an ability to adhere to vital procedures when it mattered most, to remain calm under pressure, to recognize where one needed to improvise and where one needed *not* to improvise. They understood how to function in a complex and dire situation. They recognized that it required teamwork and preparation and that it required them long before the situation became complex and dire.

This was what was unusual. This is what it means to be a hero in the modern era. These are the rare qualities that we must understand are needed in the larger world.

All learned occupations have a definition of professionalism, a code of conduct. It is where they spell out their ideals and duties. The codes are sometimes stated, sometimes just understood. But they all have at least three common elements.

First is an expectation of selflessness: that we who accept responsibility for others—whether we are doctors, lawyers, teachers, public authorities, soldiers, or pilots—will place the needs and concerns of those who depend on us above our own. Second is an expectation of skill: that we will aim for excellence in our knowledge and expertise. Third is an expectation of trustworthiness: that we will be responsible in our personal behavior toward our charges.

Aviators, however, add a fourth expectation, discipline: discipline in following prudent procedure and in functioning with others. This is a concept almost entirely outside the lexicon of most professions, including my own. In medicine, we hold up "autonomy" as a professional lodestar, a principle that stands in direct opposition to discipline. But in a world in which success now requires large enterprises, teams of clinicians, high-risk technologies, and knowledge that outstrips any one person's abilities, individual autonomy hardly seems the ideal we should aim for. It has the ring more of protectionism than of excellence. The closest our professional codes come to articulating the goal is an occasional plea for "collegiality." What is needed, however, isn't just that people working together be nice to each other. It is discipline.

Discipline is hard—harder than trustworthiness and skill and perhaps even than selflessness. We are by nature flawed and inconstant creatures. We can't even keep from snacking between meals. We are not built for discipline. We are built for novelty and excitement, not for careful attention to detail. Discipline is something we have to work at.

That's perhaps why aviation has required institutions to make discipline a norm. The preflight checklist began as an invention of a handful of army pilots in the 1930s, but the power of their discovery gave birth to entire organizations. In the United States, we now have the National Transportation Safety Board to study accidents—to independently determine the underlying causes and recommend how to remedy them. And we have national regulations to ensure that those recommendations are incorporated into usable checklists and reliably adopted in ways that actually reduce harm.

To be sure, checklists must not become ossified mandates that hinder rather than help. Even the simplest requires frequent revisitation and ongoing refinement. Airline manufacturers put a publication date on all their checklists, and there is a reason why—they are expected to change with time. In the end, a checklist is only an aid. If it doesn't aid, it's not right. But if it does, we must be ready to embrace the possibility.

We have most readily turned to the computer as our aid. Computers hold out the prospect of automation as our bulwark against failure. Indeed, they can take huge numbers of tasks off our hands, and thankfully already have—tasks of calculation, processing, storage, transmission. Without question, technology can increase our capabilities. But there is much that technology cannot do: deal with the unpredictable, manage uncertainty, construct a soaring building, perform a lifesaving operation. In many ways, technology has complicated these matters. It has added yet another element of complexity to the systems we depend on and given us entirely new kinds of failure to contend with.

One essential characteristic of modern life is that we all depend on systems—on assemblages of people or technologies or both—and among our most profound difficulties is making them work. In medicine, for instance, if I want my patients to receive the best care possible, not only must I do a good job but a whole collection of diverse components have to somehow mesh together effectively. Health care is like a car that way, points out Donald Berwick, president of the Institute for Healthcare Improvement in Boston and one of our deepest thinkers about systems in medicine. In both cases, having great components is not enough.

We're obsessed in medicine with having great components— the best drugs, the best devices, the best specialists—but pay little attention to how to make them fit together well. Berwick notes how wrongheaded this approach is. "Anyone who understands systems will know immediately that optimizing parts is not a good route to system excellence," he says. He gives the example of a famous thought experiment of trying to build the world's greatest car by assembling the world's greatest car parts. We connect the engine of a Ferrari, the brakes of a Porsche, the suspension of a BMW, the body of a Volvo. "What we get, of course, is nothing close to a great car; we get a pile of very expensive junk."

Nonetheless, in medicine that's exactly what we have done. We have a thirty-billion-dollar-a-year National Institutes of Health, which has been a remarkable powerhouse of medical discoveries. But we have no National Institute of Health Systems Innovation alongside it studying how best to incorporate these discoveries into daily practice—no NTSB equivalent swooping in to study failures the way crash investigators do, no Boeing mapping out the checklists, no agency tracking the month-to-month results.

The same can be said in numerous other fields. We don't study routine failures in teaching, in law, in government programs, in the financial industry, or elsewhere. We don't look for the patterns of our recurrent mistakes or devise and refine potential solutions for them.

But we could, and that is the ultimate point. We are all plagued by failures—by missed subtleties, overlooked knowledge, and outright errors. For the most part, we have imagined that little can be done beyond working harder and harder to catch the problems and clean up after them. We are not in the habit of thinking the way the army pilots did as they looked upon their shiny new Model 299 bomber—a machine so complex no one was sure human beings could fly it. They too could have decided just to "try harder" or to dismiss a crash as the failings of a "weak" pilot.

Instead they chose to accept their fallibilities. They recognized the simplicity and power of using a checklist.

And so can we. Indeed, against the complexity of the world, we must. There is no other choice. When we look closely, we recognize the same balls being dropped over and over, even by those of great ability and determination. We know the patterns. We see the costs. It's time to try something else.

Try a checklist.

9. THE SAVE

In the spring of 2007, as soon as our surgery checklist began taking form, I began using it in my own operations. I did so not because I thought it was needed but because I wanted to make sure it was really usable. Also, I did not want to be a hypocrite. We were about to trot this thing out in eight cities around the world. I had better be using it myself. But in my heart of hearts—if you strapped me down and threatened to take out my appendix without anesthesia unless I told the truth—did I think the checklist would make much of a difference in my cases? No. In *my* cases? Please.

To my chagrin, however, I have yet to get through a week in surgery without the checklist's leading us to catch something we would have missed. Take last week, as I write this, for instance. We had three catches in five cases.

I had a patient who hadn't gotten the antibiotic she should have received before the incision, which is one of our most common catches. The anesthesia team had gotten distracted by the usual vicissitudes. They had trouble finding a good vein for an IV, and one of the monitors was being twitchy. Then the nurse called a time-out for the team to run the Before Incision check.

"Has the antibiotic been given within the last sixty minutes?" I asked, reading my lines off a wall poster.

"Oh, right, um, yes, it will be," the anesthesia resident replied. We waited a quiet minute for the medication to flow in before the scrub tech handed over the knife.

I had another patient who specifically didn't want the antibiotic. Antibiotics give her intestinal upset and yeast infections, she said. She understood the benefits, but the risk of a bacterial wound infection in her particular operation was low—about 1 percent—and she was willing to take her chances. Yet giving an antibiotic was so automatic (when we weren't distracted from it) that we twice nearly infused it into her, despite her objections. The first time was before she went to sleep and she caught the error herself. The second time was after and the checklist caught it. As we went around the room at the pause before the incision, making sure no one had any concerns, the nurse reminded everyone not to give the antibiotic. The anesthesia attending reacted with surprise. She hadn't been there for the earlier conversation and was about to drip it in.

The third catch involved a woman in her sixties for whom I was doing a neck operation to remove half of her thyroid because of potential cancer. She'd had her share of medical problems and required a purseful of medications to keep them under control. She'd also been a longtime heavy smoker but had quit a few years before. There seemed to be no significant lingering effects. She could climb two flights of stairs without shortness of breath or chest pain. She looked generally well. Her lungs sounded clear and without wheezes under my stethoscope. The records showed no pulmonary diagnoses. But when she met the anesthesiologist before surgery, she remembered that she'd had trouble breathing after two previous operations and had required oxygen at home for several weeks. In one instance, she'd required a stay in intensive care.

This was a serious concern. The anesthesiologist knew about it, but I didn't—not until we ran the checklist. When the moment came to raise concerns, the anesthesiologist asked why I wasn't planning to watch her longer than the usual few hours after day surgery, given her previous respiratory problems.

"What respiratory problems?" I said. The full story came out from there. We made arrangements to keep the patient in the hospital for observation. Moreover, we made plans to give her inhalers during surgery and afterward to prevent breathing problems. They worked beautifully. She never needed extra oxygen at all.

No matter how routine an operation is, the patients never seem to be. But with the checklist in place, we have caught unrecognized drug allergies, equipment problems, confusion about medications, mistakes on labels for biopsy specimens going to pathology. ("No, *that* one is from the right side. This is the one from the left side.") We've made better plans and been better prepared for patients. I am not sure how many important issues would have slipped by us without the checklist and actually caused harm. We were not bereft of defenses. Our usual effort to be vigilant and attentive might have caught some of the problems. And those we didn't catch may never have gone on to hurt anyone.

I had one case, however, in which I know for sure the checklist saved my patient's life. Mr. Hagerman, as we'll call him, was a fifty-three-year-old father of two and the CEO of a local company, and I had brought him to the operating room to remove his right adrenal gland because of an unusual tumor growing inside it called a pheochromocytoma. Tumors like his pour out dangerous levels of adrenalin and can be difficult to remove. They are also exceedingly rare. But in recent years, I've developed alongside my general surgery practice a particular interest and expertise in endocrine surgery. I've now removed somewhere around forty adrenal tumors without complication. So when Mr. Hagerman came to see me about this strange mass in his right adrenal gland, I felt quite confident about my ability to help him. There is always a risk of serious complications, I explained—the primary danger occurs when you're taking the gland off the vena cava, the main vessel returning blood to the heart, because injuring the vena cava can cause life-threatening bleeding. But the likelihood was low, I reassured him.

Once you're in the operating room, however, you either have a complication or you don't. And with him I did.

I was doing the operation laparoscopically, freeing the tumor with instruments I observed on a video monitor using a fiberoptic camera we put inside Mr. Hagerman. All was going smoothly. I was able to lift the liver up and out of the way, and underneath I found the soft, tan yellow mass, like the yolk of a hard-boiled egg. I began dissecting it free of the vena cava, and although doing so was painstaking, it didn't seem unusually difficult. I'd gotten the tumor mostly separated when I did something I'd never done before: I made a tear in the vena cava.

This is a catastrophe. I might as well have made a hole directly in Mr. Hagerman's heart. The bleeding that resulted was terrifying. He lost almost his entire volume of blood into his abdomen in about sixty seconds and went into cardiac arrest. I made a huge slashing incision to open his chest and belly as fast and wide as I could. I took his heart in my hand and began compressing it—one-two-three-squeeze, one-two-three-squeeze—to keep his blood flow going to his brain. The resident assisting me held pressure on the vena cava to slow the torrent. But in the grip of my fingers, I could feel the heart emptying out.

I thought it was over, that we'd never get Mr. Hagerman out of the operating room alive, that I had killed him. But we had run the checklist at the start of the case. When we had come to the part where I was supposed to discuss how much blood loss the team should be prepared for, I said, "I don't expect much blood loss. I've never lost more than one hundred cc's." I was confident. I was looking forward to this operation. But I added that the tumor was pressed right up against the vena cava and that significant blood loss remained at least a theoretical concern. The nurse took that as a cue to check that four units of packed red cells had been set aside in the blood bank, like they were supposed to be—"just in case," as she said.

They hadn't been, it turned out. So the blood bank got the four units ready. And as a result, from this one step alone, the checklist saved my patient's life.

Just as powerful, though, was the effect that the routine of the checklist—the discipline—had on us. Of all the people in the room as we started that operation—the anesthesiologist, the nurse anesthetist, the surgery resident, the scrub nurse, the circulating nurse, the medical student—I had worked with only two before, and I knew only the resident well. But as we went around the room introducing ourselves—"Atul Gawande, surgeon." "Rich Bafford, surgery resident." "Sue Marchand, nurse"—you could feel the room snapping to attention. We confirmed the patient's name on his ID bracelet and that we all agreed which adrenal gland was supposed to come out. The anesthesiologist confirmed that he had no critical issues to mention before starting, and so did the nurses. We made sure that the antibiotics were in the patient, a warming blanket was on his body, the inflating boots were on his legs to keep blood clots from developing. We came into the room as strangers. But when the knife hit the skin, we were a team.

As a result, when I made the tear and put disaster upon us, everyone kept their head. The circulating nurse called an alarm for extra personnel and got the blood from the blood bank almost instantly. The anesthesiologist began pouring unit after unit into the patient. Forces were marshaled to bring in the additional equipment I requested, to page the vascular surgeon I wanted, to assist the anesthesiologist with obtaining more intravenous access, to keep the blood bank apprised. And together the team got me—and the patient—precious time. They ended up transfusing more than thirty units of blood into him—he lost three times as much blood as his body contained to begin with. And with our eyes on the monitor tracing his blood pressure and my hand squeezing his heart, it proved enough to keep his circulation going. The vascular surgeon and I had time to work out an effective way to clamp off the vena cava tear. I could feel his heart begin beating on its own again. We were able to put in sutures and close the hole. And Mr. Hagerman survived.

I cannot pretend he escaped unscathed. The extended period of low blood pressure damaged an optic nerve and left him essentially blind in one eye. He didn't get off the respirator for days. He was out of work for months. I was crushed by what I had put him through. Though I apologized to him and carried on with my daily routine, it took me a long time to feel right again in surgery. I can't do an adrenalectomy without thinking of his case, and I suspect that is good. I have even tried refining the operative technique in hopes of coming up with better ways to protect the vena cava and keep anything like his experience from happening again.

But more than this, because of Mr. Hagerman's operation, I have come to be grateful for what a checklist can do. I do not like to think how much worse the case could have been. I do not like to think about having to walk out to that family waiting area and explain to his wife that her husband had died.

I spoke to Mr. Hagerman not long ago. He had sold his company with great success and was in the process of turning another company around. He was running three days a week. He was even driving.

"I have to watch out for my blind spot, but I can manage," he said.

He had no bitterness, no anger, and this is remarkable to me. "I count myself lucky just to be alive," he insisted. I asked him if I could have permission to tell others his story.

"Yes," he said. "I'd be glad if you did."

NOTES ON SOURCES

INTRODUCTION

7 "In the 1970s": S. Gorovitz and A. MacIntyre, "Toward a Theory of Medical Fallibility," *Journal of Medicine and Philosophy* 1 (1976): 51–71.

9 "The first safe medication": M. Hamilton and E. N. Thompson, "The Role of Blood Pressure Control in Preventing Complications of Hypertension," *Lancet* 1 (1964): 235–39. See also VA Cooperative Study Group, "Effects of Treatment on Morbidity of Hypertension," *Journal of the American Medical Association* 202 (1967): 1028–33.

10 "After that, survival": R. L. McNamara et al., "Effect of Door-to-Balloon Time on Mortality in Patients with ST-Segment Elevation Myocardial Infarction," *Journal of the American College of Cardiology* 47 (2006): 2180–86.

10 "In 2006": E. H. Bradley et al., "Strategies for Reducing the Door-to-Balloon Time in Acute Myocardial Infarction," *New England Journal of Medicine* 355 (2006): 2308–20.

10 "Studies have found": E. A. McGlynn et al., "Rand Research Brief: The First National Report Card on Quality of Health Care in America," Rand Corporation, 2006.

11 "You see it in the 36 percent increase": American Bar Association, *Profile of Legal Malpractice Claims, 2004–2007* (Chicago: American Bar Association, 2008).

1. THE PROBLEM OF EXTREME COMPLEXITY

15 "I read a case report": M. Thalmann, N. Trampitsch, M. Haberfellner, et al., "Resuscitation in Near Drowning with Extracorporeal Membrane Oxygenation," *Annals of Thoracic Surgery* 72 (2001): 607–8.

21 "The answer that came back": Further details of the analysis by Marcus Semel, Richard Marshall, and Amy Marston will appear in a forthcoming scientific article.

23 "On any given day": Society of Critical Care Medicine, Critical Care Statistics in the United States, 2006.

23 "The average stay": J. E. Zimmerman et al., "Intensive Care Unit Length of Stay: Benchmarking Based on Acute Physiology and Chronic Health Evaluation (APACHE) IV," *Critical Care Medicine* 34 (2006): 2517–29.

23 "Fifteen years ago": Y. Donchin et al., "A Look into the Nature and Causes of Human Errors in the Intensive Care Unit," *Critical Care Medicine* 23 (1995): 294–300.

24 "There are dangers simply": N. Vaecker et al., "Bone Resorption Is Induced on the Second Day of Bed Rest: Results of a Controlled, Crossover Trial," *Journal of Applied Physiology* 95 (2003): 977–82.

28 "national statistics show": Centers for Disease Control, "National Nosocomial Infection Surveillance (NNIS) System Report, 2004, Data Summary from January 1992 through June 2004, Issued October 2004," *American Journal of Infection Control* 32 (2004): 470–85.

28 "Those who survive line infections": P. Kalfon et al., "Comparison of Silver-Impregnated with Standard Multi-Lumen Central Venous Catheters in Critically Ill Patients," *Critical Care Medicine* 35 (2007): 1032–39.

28 "All in all, about half": S. Ghorra et al., "Analysis of the Effect of Conversion from Open to Closed Surgical Intensive Care Units," *Annals of Surgery* 2 (1999): 163–71.

2. THE CHECKLIST

32 "On October 30, 1935": P. S. Meilinger, "When the Fortress Went Down," *Air Force Magazine*, Oct. 2004, pp. 78–82.

35 "A study of forty-one thousand": J. R. Clarke, A. V. Ragone, and L. Greenwald, "Comparisons of Survival Predictions Using Survival Risk Ratios Based on International Classification of Diseases, Ninth Revision and Abbreviated Injury Scale Trauma Diagnosis Codes," *Journal of Trauma* 59 (2005): 563–69.

35 "Practitioners have had the means": J. V. Stewart, *Vital Signs and Resuscitation* (Georgetown, TX: Landes Bioscience, 2003).

38 "In more than a third of patients": S. M. Berenholtz et al., "Eliminating Catheter-Related Bloodstream Infections in the Intensive Care Unit," *Critical Care Medicine* 32 (2004): 2014–20.

39 "This reduced from 41 percent": M. A. Erdek and P. J. Pronovost, "Improvement of Assessment and Treatment of Pain in the Critically Ill," *International Journal for Quality Improvement in Healthcare* 16 (2004): 59–64.

39 "The proportion of patients": S. M. Berenholtz et al., "Improving Care for the Ventilated Patient," *Joint Commission Journal on Quality and Safety* 4 (2004): 195–204.

39 "The researchers found": P. J. Pronovost et al., "Improving Communication in the ICU Using Daily Goals," *Journal of Critical Care* 18 (2003): 71–75.

39 "In a survey of ICU staff": Berenholtz et al., "Improving Care."

41 "But between 2000 and 2003": K. Norris, "DMC Ends 2004 in the Black, but Storm Clouds Linger," *Detroit Free Press*, March 30, 2005.

44 "In December 2006": P. J. Pronovost et al., "An Intervention to Reduce Catheter-Related Bloodstream Infections in the ICU," *New England Journal of Medicine* 355 (2006): 2725–32.

3. THE END OF THE MASTER BUILDER

48 "Two professors who study": S. Glouberman and B. Zimmerman, "Complicated and Complex Systems: What Would Successful Reform of Medicare Look Like?" discussion paper no. 8, Commission on the Future of Health Care in Canada, Saskatoon, 2002.

54 "His firm, McNamara / Salvia": Portfolio at www.mcsal.com.

59 "We've been slow to adapt": Data from the *Dartmouth Atlas of Health Care*, www.darmouthatlas.org.

69 "It was planned to rise": R. J. McNamara, "Robert J. McNamara, SE, FASCE," *Structural Design of Tall and Special Buildings* 17 (2008): 493–512.

70 "But, as a *New Yorker* story": Joe Morgenstern, "The Fifty-Nine-Story Crisis," *New Yorker*, May 29, 1995.

71 "In the United States": U.S. Census data for 2003 and 2008, www .census.gov; K. Wardhana and F. C. Hadipriono, "Study of Recent Building Failures in the United States," *Journal of Performance of Constructed Facilities* 17 (2003): 151–58.

4. THE IDEA

73 "At 6:00 a.m.": Hurricane Katrina events and data from E. Scott, "Hurricane Katrina," *Managing Crises: Responses to Large-Scale Emergencies*, ed. A. M. Howitt and H. B. Leonard (Washington, D.C.: CQ Press, 2009), pp. 13–74.

76 "Of all organizations": Wal-Mart events and data from S. Rosegrant, "Wal-Mart's Response to Hurricane Katrina," *Managing Crises*, pp. 379–406.

78 "For every Wal-Mart": D. Gross, "What FEMA Could Learn from Wal-Mart: Less Than You Think," *Slate*, Sept. 23, 2005, http:// www.slate.com/id/2126832.

78 "In the early days": Scott, "Hurricane Katrina," p. 49.

80 "As Roth explained": D. L. Roth, *Crazy from the Heat* (New York: Hyperion, 1997).

81 "Her focus is on regional Italian cuisine": J. Adams and K. Rivard, *In the Hands of a Chef: Cooking with Jody Adams of Rialto Restaurant* (New York: William Morrow, 2002).

5. THE FIRST TRY

87 "By 2004": T. G. Weiser et al., "An Estimation of the Global Volume of Surgery: A Modelling Strategy Based on Available Data," *Lancet* 372 (2008): 139–44.

87 "Although most of the time": A. A. Gawande et al., "The Incidence and Nature of Surgical Adverse Events in Colorado and Utah in 1992," *Surgery* 126 (1999): 66–75.

87 "Worldwide, at least seven million people": Weiser, "An Estimation," and World Health Organization, *World Health Report, 2004* (Geneva: WHO, 2004). See annex, table 2.

91 "The strategy has shown results": P. K. Lindenauer et al., "Public Reporting and Pay for Performance in Hospital Quality Improvement," *New England Journal of Medicine* 356 (2007): 486–96.

93 "When the disease struck": S. Johnson, *The Ghost Map* (New York: Riverhead, 2006).

95 "Luby and his team reported": S. P. Luby et al., "Effect of Handwashing on Child Health: A Randomised Controlled Trial," *Lancet* 366 (2005): 225–33.

98 "But give it on time": A. A. Gawande and T. G. Weiser, eds., *World Health Organization Guidelines for Safe Surgery* (Geneva: WHO, 2008).

102 "In one survey of three hundred": M. A. Makary et al., "Operating Room Briefings and Wrong-Site Surgery," *Journal of the American College of Surgeons* 204 (2007): 236–43.

102 "surveyed more than a thousand": J. B. Sexton, E. J. Thomas, and R. L. Helmsreich, "Error, Stress, and Teamwork in Medicine and Aviation," *British Medical Journal* 320 (2000): 745–49.

108 "The researchers learned": See preliminary data reported in "Team Communication in Safety," *OR Manager* 19, no. 12 (2003): 3.

109 "After three months": Makary et al., "Operating Room Briefings and Wrong-Site Surgery."

109 "At the Kaiser hospitals": " 'Preflight Checklist' Builds Safety Culture, Reduces Nurse Turnover," *OR Manager* 19, no. 12 (2003): 1–4.

109 "At Toronto": L. Lingard et al. "Getting Teams to Talk: Development and Prior Implementation of a Checklist to Promote Interpersonal Communication in the OR," *Quality and Safety in Health Care* 14 (2005): 340–46.

6. THE CHECKLIST FACTORY

114 "Among the articles I found": D. J. Boorman, "Reducing Flight Crew Errors and Minimizing New Error Modes with Electronic Checklists," *Proceedings of the International Conference on Human-Computer Interaction in Aeronautics* (Toulouse: Editions Cépaudès, 2000), pp. 57–63; D. J. Boorman, "Today's Electronic Checklists Reduce Likelihood of Crew Errors and Help Prevent Mishaps," *ICAO Journal* 56 (2001): 17–20.

116 "An electrical short": National Traffic Safety Board, "Aircraft Accident Report: Explosive Decompression—Loss of Cargo Door in Flight, United Airlines Flight 811, Boeing 747-122, N4713U, Honolulu, Hawaii, February 24, 1989," Washington D.C., March 18, 1992.

116 "The plane was climbing": S. White, "Twenty-Six Minutes of Terror," *Flight Safety Australia*, Nov.–Dec. 1999, pp. 40–42.

120 "They can help experts": A. Degani and E. L.Wiener, "Human Factors of Flight-Deck Checklists: The Normal Checklist," NASA Contractor Report 177549, Ames Research Center, May 1990.

121 "Some have been found confusing": Aviation Safety Reporting System, "ASRS Database Report Set: Checklist Incidents," 2009.

129 "Crash investigators with Britain's": Air Accidents Investigation Branch, "AAIB Interim Report: Accident to Boeing 777-236ER,

G-YMMM, at London Heathrow Airport on 17 January 2008," Department of Transport, London, Sept. 2008.

129 " 'It was just yards above' ": M. Fricker, "Gordon Brown Just 25 Feet from Death in Heathrow Crash," *Daily Mirror*, Jan. 18, 2008.

129 "The nose wheels collapsed": Air Accidents Investigation Branch, "AAIB Bulletin S1/2008," Department of Transport, London, Feb. 2008.

130 "Their initial reports": Air Accidents Investigation Branch, "AAIB Bulletin S1/2008"; Air Accidents Investigation Branch, "AAIB Bulletin S3/2008," Department of Transport, London, May 2008.

132 "Nonetheless, the investigators tested": Air Accidents Investigation Branch, "AAIB Interim Report."

132 "So in September 2008": Federal Aviation Administration, Airworthiness Directive; Boeing Model 777-200 and -300 Series Airplanes Equipped with Rolls-Royce Model RB211-TRENT 800 Series Engines, Washington, D.C., Sept. 12, 2008.

133 "One study in medicine": E. A. Balas and S. A. Boren, "Managing Clinical Knowledge for Health Care Improvement," *Yearbook of Medical Informatics* (2000): 65–70.

133 "almost 700,000 medical journal articles": National Library of Medicine, "Key Medline Indicators," Nov. 12, 2008, accessed at www.nlm.nih.gov/bsd/bsd_key.html.

134 "This time it was": National Transportation Safety Board, "Safety Recommendations A-09-17-18," Washington, D.C., March 11, 2009.

7. THE TEST

139 "Of the tens of millions": Joint Commission, Sentinel Event Alert, June 24, 2003.

139 "By comparison, some 300,000": R. D. Scott, "The Direct Medical Costs of Healthcare-Associated Infections in U.S. Hospitals and the Benefits of Prevention," Centers for Disease Control, March 2009.

140 "The final WHO safe surgery checklist": The checklist can be accessed at www.who.int/safesurgery.

146 "We gave them some PowerPoint slides": The videos can be viewed at www.safesurg.org/materials.html.

156 "In January 2009": A. B. Haynes et al., "A Surgical Safety Checklist to Reduce Morbidity and Mortality in a Global Population," *New England Journal of Medicine* 360 (2009): 491–99.

8. THE HERO IN THE AGE OF CHECKLISTS

161 "Tom Wolfe's *The Right Stuff*": T. Wolfe, *The Right Stuff* (New York: Farrar, Straus and Giroux, 1979).

163 "Neuroscientists have found": H. Breiter et al., "Functional Imaging of Neural Responses to Expectancy and Experience of Monetary Gains and Losses," *Neuron* 30 (2001): 619–39.

166 "'Cort's earning power'": Wesco Financial Corporation, Securities and Exchange Commission, Form 8-K filing, May 4, 2005.

170 "Smart specifically studied": G. H. Smart, "Management Assessment Methods in Venture Capital: An Empirical Analysis of Human Capital Valuation," *Journal of Private Equity* 2, no. 3 (1999): 29–45.

172 "He has since gone on": G. H. Smart and R. Street, *Who: The A Method for Hiring* (New York: Ballantine, 2008).

173 "A National Transportation Safety Board official": J. Olshan and I. Livingston, "Quiet Air Hero Is Captain America," *New York Post*, Jan. 17, 2009.

174 "As Sullenberger kept saying": M. Phillips, "Sully, Flight 1549 Crew Receive Keys to New York City," The Middle Seat, blog, *Wall Street Journal*, Feb. 9, 2009, http://blogs.wsj.com/middleseat/2009/02/09/.

174 "'That was so long ago'": "Sully's Tale," *Air & Space*, Feb. 18, 2009.

178 "Once that happened": C. Sullenberger and J. Zaslow, *Highest Duty: My Search for What Really Matters* (New York: William Morrow, 2009).

179 "Skiles managed to complete": Testimony of Captain Terry Lutz, Experimental Test Pilot, Engineering Flight Operations, Airbus,

National Transportation Safety Board, "Public Hearing in the Matter of the Landing of US Air Flight 1549 in the Hudson River, Weehawken, New Jersey, January 15, 2009," June 10, 2009.

180 " 'Flaps out?' ": D. P. Brazy, "Group Chairman's Factual Report of Investigation: Cockpit Voice Recorder DCA09MA026," National Transportation Safety Board, April 22, 2009.

180 "For, as journalist and pilot": W. Langewiesche, "Anatomy of a Miracle," *Vanity Fair*, June 2009.

181 "After the plane landed": Testimony of Captain Chesley Sullenberger, A320 Captain, US Airways, National Transportation Safety Board, Public Hearing, June 9, 2009.

ACKNOWLEDGMENTS

Three kinds of people were pivotal to this book: the ones behind the writing, the ones behind the ideas, and the ones who made both possible. As the book involved background research in several fields beyond my expertise, the number of people I am indebted to is especially large. But this book could never have been completed without all of them.

First are those who helped me take my loose observations about failure and checklists and bring them together in book form. My agent, Tina Bennett, saw the possibilities right away and championed the book from the moment I first told her about my burgeoning fascination with checklists. My editor at the *New Yorker*, the indispensable Henry Finder, showed me how to give my initial draft more structure and my thinking more coherence.

Laura Schoenherr, my brilliant and indefatigable research assistant, found almost every source here, checked my facts, provided suggestions, and kept me honest. Roslyn Schloss provided meticulous copyediting and a vital final review. At Metropolitan Books, Riva Hocherman went through the text with inspired intelligence and gave crucial advice at every stage of the book's development. Most of all, I leaned on Sara Bershtel, Metropolitan's publisher, with whom I've worked for nearly a decade now. Smart, tough, and tireless, she combed through multiple drafts, got me to sharpen every section, and saved me from numerous errors of tone and thinking, all the while shepherding the book through production with almost alarming efficiency.

As for the underlying ideas and the stories and experience fleshing them out, I have many, many to thank. Donald Berwick taught me the science of systems improvement and opened my eyes to the possibilities of checklists in medicine. Peter Pronovost provided a crucial source of ideas with his seminal work in ICUs. Lucian Leape, David Bates, and Berwick were the ones to suggest my name to the World Health Organization. Sir Liam Donaldson, the chair of WHO Patient Safety, who established the organization's global campaign to reduce deaths in surgery, was kind enough to bring me aboard to lead it and then showed me what leadership in public health really meant. Pauline Philip, the executive director of WHO Patient Safety, didn't take no for an answer from me and proved extraordinary in both her dedication and her effectiveness in carrying out work that has now extended across dozens of countries.

At WHO, Margaret Chan, the director general, as well as Ian Smith, her adviser, David Heymann, deputy director general, and

Tim Evans, assistant director general, have all been stalwart supporters. I am also particularly grateful to Gerald Dziekan, whom I have worked with almost daily for the past three years, and also Vivienne Allan, Hilary Coates, Armorel Duncan, Helen Hughes, Sooyeon Hwang, Angela Lashoher, Claire Lemer, Agnes Leotsakos, Pat Martin, Douglas Noble, Kristine Stave, Fiona Stewart-Mills, and Julie Storr.

At Boeing, Daniel Boorman emerged as an essential partner in work that has now extended to designing, testing, and implementing clinical checklists for safe childbirth, control of diarrheal infections, operating room crises, management of patients with H1N1 influenza, and other areas. Jamie and Christopher Cooper-Hohn, Roman Emmanuel, Mala Gaonkar and Oliver Haarmann, David Greenspan, and Yen and Eeling Liow were early and vital backers.

At the Harvard School of Public Health, the trio of William Berry, Tom Weiser, and Alex Haynes have been the steel columns of the surgery checklist work. The WHO Safe Surgery program I describe in this book also depended on Abdel-Hadi Breizat, Lord Ara Darzi, E. Patchen Dellinger, Teodoro Herbosa, Sidhir Joseph, Pascience Kibatala, Marie Lapitan, Alan Merry, Krishna Moorthy, Richard Reznick, and Bryce Taylor, the principal investigators at our eight study sites around the world; Bruce Barraclough, Martin Makary, Didier Pittet, and Iskander Sayek, the leaders of our scientific advisory group, as well as the many participants in the WHO Safe Surgery Saves Lives study group; Martin Fletcher and Lord Naren Patel at the National Patient Safety Agency in the U.K.; Alex Arriaga, Angela Bader, Kelly Bernier, Bridget Craig, Priya Desai, Rachel Dyer, Lizzie Edmondson,

Luke Funk, Stuart Lipsitz, Scott Regenbogen, and my colleagues at the Brigham and Women's Center for Surgery and Public Health; and the MacArthur Foundation.

I am deeply indebted to the many experts named throughout the book whose generosity and forbearance helped me explore their fields. Unnamed here are Jonathan Katz, who opened the door to the world of skyscraper building; Dutch Leonard and Arnold Howitt, who explained Hurricane Katrina to me; Nuno Alvez and Andrew Hebert, Rialto's sous chefs, who let me invade their kitchen; Eugene Hill, who sent me the work of Geoff Smart; and Marcus Semel, the research fellow in my group who analyzed the data from Harvard Vanguard Medical Associates showing the complexity of clinical work in medicine and the national data showing the frequency of death in surgery. In addition, Katy Thompson helped me with the research and fact-checking behind my *New Yorker* article "The Checklist," which this book grew out of.

Lastly, we come to those without whom my life in writing and research and surgery would be impossible. Elizabeth Morse, my administrative director, has proved irreplaceable, lending a level head, around-the-clock support, and continually wise counsel. Michael Zinner, the chairman of my surgery department at Brigham and Women's Hospital, and Arnie Epstein, the chairman of my health policy and management department at the Harvard School of Public Health, have backed me in this project as they have for many others over the last decade and more. David Remnick, the editor of the *New Yorker*, has been nothing but kind and loyal, keeping me on staff through this entire period. I could not be more fortunate to have such extraordinary people behind me.

Most important, however, are two final groups. There are my

patients, both those who have let me tell their stories here and those who have simply trusted me to try to help with their care. I have learned more from them than from anyone else. And then there is my family. My wife, Kathleen, and children, Hunter, Hattie, and Walker, tend to suffer the brunt of my mutating commitments and enthusiasms. But they have always found ways to make room for my work, to share in it, and to remind me that it is not everything. My thanks to them are boundless.